Red, White and Tuna

by
Jaston Williams   Joe Sears   Ed Howard

A SAMUEL FRENCH ACTING EDITION

SAMUEL FRENCH

FOUNDED 1830

NEW YORK HOLLYWOOD LONDON TORONTO

SAMUELFRENCH.COM

ISBN 978-0-573-69673-2   Printed in U.S.A.   #29081

MUSIC USE NOTE

IMPORTANT BILLING AND CREDIT
REQUIREMENTS

Originally Produced by Charles Duggan

RED, WHITE AND TUNA had its world premiere at the 1894 Grand Opera House in Galveston Island, Texas on April 7, 1998. The play was produced by Charles H. Duggan, (Producing Associates – Carla McQueen and Joe Mac) and directed by Ed Howard. Sets were by Kevin Rupnik, costumes were by Linda Fisher, sound was by Ken Huncovsky and lighting was by Root Choyce. The production stage manager was Robert Tolaro. All roles were played by Joe Sears and Jaston Williams.

CHARACTER DESCRIPTIONS

When all characters are played by two actors, one actor plays:

STAR BIRDFEATHER – A flower child.

THURSTON WHEELIS – A radio disc jockey.

ELMER WATKINS – A veteran Klan member.

BERTHA BUMILLER – A widowed housewife and mother.

JOE BOB LIPSEY – The artistic director of the Tuna Little Theatre.

PEARL BURRAS – Bertha's aunt, a chicken farmer.

R. R. SNAVELY – Estranged husband of gun shop owner Didi Snavely.

INITA GOODWIN – The half-owner of Hot to Trot Catering.

LEONARD CHILDERS – Tuna's mayor and owner of radio station OKKK.

REVEREND STURGIS SPIKES – A Baptist preacher.

When all characters are played by two actors, the other actor plays:

AMBER WINDCHIME – Star's friend, another flower child.

ARLES STRUVIE – A radio disc jockey.

DIDI SNAVELY – Used gun store owner.

PETEY FISK – Head of Tuna's Humane Society.

MOMMA BYRD – Didi's ancient mother, an off-stage voice.

CHARLENE BUMILLER – Bertha's pregnant daughter.

STANLEY BUMILLER – Bertha's son, a reformed juvenile delinquent and artist.

VERA CARP – Head of Tuna society.

HELEN BEDD – The other half-owner of Hot to Trot Catering.

GARLAND POTEET – A soda pop delivery man.

ACT I

Scene One

(As the lights come up **STAR BIRDFEATHER** *and* **AMBER WINDCHIME,** *two aging hippies, are seated in two chairs which comprise the front seat of Star's Volkswagen Beetle.)*

AMBER. Oh, no. Star, did we forget to pack the tofu sausage?

STAR. Amber, I'm so sorry. I scarfed it outside of San Angelo while you were sleeping.

AMBER. Don't worry, Star, that Echinacea shake will tide me over.

STAR. Amber, are you sure we did the right thing?

AMBER. Only packing one pound of dried edamame?

STAR. No, I mean going back to Tuna to our high school reunion. Maybe we should have headed back to Montana to the "Save the Wolverines" convocation.

AMBER. Star, I don't want to be, like, a downer, but it's pretty clear from their attitude that the wolverines don't want to be saved.

STAR. Yeah, that was so heavy when they ate the tires off the Winnebago.

AMBER. Talk about hostile.

STAR. But Amber, don't you think we have to keep trying?

AMBER. We did. That was the whole point last year of providing anti-depressants to the wolverines, and they ate the tires off the Winnebago again.

STAR. Yeah, it just took them longer.

AMBER. I mean, I'm as spiritual as the next person, but I maxed out my Visa card on those tires. I'm ready to start an organization that's called, "Screw the Wolverines."

*(**AMBER** begins a ritual of putting Patchouli on her wrists and eye drops in her eyes.)*

STAR. I'm sorry, Amber. I guess I'm a little freaked out going back into carnivore territory. I'm just afraid I'll throw up my toenails at the sight of dead animal on white bread.

AMBER. Just remember that guy from California and be here now.

STAR. But what if nobody calls us by our new names?

AMBER. We just have to channel that blond chick from Seattle and bask in the refuge of the white light.

STAR. But it's different for you. You had a cool organic name like Fern. I'd rather eat a sloppy joe than answer to Bernice.

AMBER. You just have to think of that guy from Mexico and realize nothing is personal even if somebody comes at you with an axe.

STAR. But Amber, what if they call us Fernie and Bernie like the old days.

AMBER. Oh, I'll kick somebody's ass.

*(**STAR** hits the brakes, bringing the car to a screeching halt.)*

STAR. Amber, take my hand. *(They hold hands.)* On three. One, two, three.

(both chanting)

Hummmmmmm. Reach out in the darkness.

AMBER. I'm generating light.

STAR. Hop on the peace train.

AMBER. All aboard.

STAR. These boots are made for walking.

AMBER. *(laughing hysterically and breaking the chant)* Star, Nancy Sinatra is not cosmic.

STAR. I know. I just couldn't think of anybody else.

AMBER. Chill, Star. I'm back, I'm balanced, I feel centered in my solar plexus.

(STAR switches to first and starts back out.)

STAR. That is so vital.

AMBER. I hate to be a downer, but I hope Connie Carp doesn't show.

STAR. Just leave her to her karma.

AMBER. I just wish her karma would hurry up.

STAR. Amber, you can't waste your white light on a spiritually bankrupt flesh munching sweat hog like Connie Carp. If you see her just walk away, René.

AMBER. I better write that down.

(She does; **STAR** *notices something they're passing by, which is Tuna, pulls over and stops the car, breaks out a joint and lights it.)*

Star, it was a really good idea to drive back to Tuna after dark so we could miss the scenery.

STAR. It's the only way. I hope Stanley Bumiller makes it home.

AMBER. Oh, he was way cool.

STAR. It always bothered me that they sent him to reform school. That wasn't fair.

AMBER. At least it got him out of P.E.

STAR. He's like super rich now.

AMBER. Oh, yeah. Remember when we saw his neo-whatever spray-paint taxidermy art show in Reno, and how moved we were? I mean, you can't get much more organic than working with real animals, even if they are dead.

STAR. It's the ultimate in recycling.

AMBER. Way cool. What a rush it was to see all those spray painted animals in costumes with their fangs bared.

STAR. Yeah. It reminded me of why we all quit doing LSD.

AMBER. You got that right.

(Pause, the sun begins to rise.)

STAR. Amber, maybe we should get out.

AMBER. Oh, Star, I don't like the looks of this.

STAR. Why, does it look different?

AMBER. No.

STAR. Let's try the radio.

Scene Two

(STAR turns the car radio on as the lights go to black, except for the light inside the onstage radio. AMBER changes to ARLES; STAR changes to THURSTON. A poorly sung version of "Texas, Our Texas" is sung. This is followed by the voice of Arles. THURSTON and ARLES enter in the dark.)

VOICE OF ARLES. *(on the radio)* This is radio station OKKK in Tuna, Texas, serving the Greater Tuna area at 275 watts signing on.

(Lights come up on THURSTON and ARLES at Radio Station OKKK.)

THURSTON. Happy Birthday, America, this is Thurston Wheelis.

ARLES. And this is Arles Struvie.

THURSTON. And this is the Wheelis...

ARLES. ...Struvie Independence Day Report. And here we go with the news. Take it away, Thurston.

THURSTON. Well, folks, it's a big day here in Tuna, but Arles, it looks like we're down to only one remaining candidate for the Tuna High School Annual Fourth-of-July Reunion Queen.

ARLES. We are?

THURSTON. We are.

ARLES. We are. We are.

THURSTON. Didi Snavely has just this morning informed me that she's dropping out of the competition

ARLES. No.

THURSTON. Yes. She say's she's no longer able to compete with Vera Carp's bulging campaign war chest, and Pearl Burras threw in the towel last night calling Vera a dirty campaigner, accused her of stealing yard signs and implying that Pearl's cage-free chickens were spreading Asian bird flu.

ARLES. Well, politics is mean in Texas. It is.

THURSTON. It is.

ARLES. It is. It is.

THURSTON. For her own part Vera's campaign focused on family values with a platform opposing stem cells, same sex marriage and calling for bans on the music of Madonna, anybody named Jackson, and Anna Maria Alberghetti.

ARLES. I've got a statement here from the Carp campaign where Vera categorically refutes the accusation that she went negative first. Vera says she thinks the voters will be more comfortable with a queen who's never been divorced or abandoned by a drunken husband and will be more than willing for Pearl and Didi to ride on her float on smaller hay bales at her feet. Nobody compares to Vera when it comes to generosity. They don't.

THURSTON. They don't.

ARLES. They don't. They don't.

THURSTON. She won't let them.

ARLES. And speaking of Didi, her husband, R.R., has one more day to come home. As you all know, R.R. disappeared several years ago and Didi gave him two thousand days to come home, or she said despite her Baptist upbringing she'd divorce him. R.R. claimed on several occasions to see UFO's and some folks think he left on one, but Didi says she can't wait any longer and will be available for dates as soon as the divorce is final, or he's declared legally dead, whichever comes first. I tell you, I hope she has an easier divorce than I did. My ex-wife Trudy lied about her age. Till I filed for divorce I didn't know she had fifteen years on me. And she got mad as hell when I brought it up on the air.

THURSTON. What did she do?

ARLES. She locked me in the trailer house and screamed, "Tornado!"

THURSTON. I remember that now.

ARLES. I can't even watch "The Wizard of Oz" without breaking out in hives. Trudy, if you're out there listening, I'll never forget you, but I won't stop trying.

*(***ARLES*** laughs as **THURSTON** exits and changes to* **ELMER WATKINS.***)*

I won't stop trying. Now, folks, it's time for a public service announcement from Tuna's own concerned citizen, Elmer Watkins. Elmer.

*(***ELMER*** enters.)*

ELMER. This is Elmer Watkins speaking to you as president of the independent nation of Free White Texas, reminding you that the Free White Texas Fourth-of-July Rally will be held on July Fifth. Now that's because we men always have a few snorts on the fourth and the wives are tired of chasing after the kids and putting out grass fires. Last year my wife put out so many fires she smelled like smoke for a month. I had nightmares about hams. It was scary. So we'll see all of you at the July 4th rally on July 5th. This is Elmer Watkins for the independent nation of Free White Texas. Thank you.

*(***ELMER*** exits and changes to* **THURSTON.** **THURSTON** *enters during below.))*

ARLES. Thank you, Elmer. And folks, on the local theatrical scene, Tuna's own little theatre director, Joe Bob Lipsey has just returned to town from directing the Big Thicket Arts Festival, where his most recent production was a musical version of Oedipus Rex called Mother's Boy. Joe Bob is back in town directing a patriotic performance art extravaganza titled Red, White and Fabulous. The show consists of famous characters in American history singing show tunes. We'll see Clyde Busby as Richard Nixon singing "Send in the clowns"; Lavita Posey will be Nancy Reagan on the morning of George Bush's inauguration singing "I'm telling you I'm not going." And who could miss Corky Burkhalter as Bill Clinton singing, "Once I Had a Secret Love"? And folks on a personal note it's true that yours truly will be tying the knot tomorrow after-noon with my dearest baby Bertha Bumiller down at the home of W.H. and Vera Carp here in Tuna. Vera has requested that only close family be in attendance at the wedding due to the high quality of her carpets and the fact that too much in and out let's the house fill up with horse flies. We are registered for wedding gifts at Didi's Used Weapons here in Tuna.

THURSTON. Now I have a question for all you listeners out there. Why would Petey Fisk of the local Humane Soci-ety agree to spend five hours inside a clear Plexiglas hut with fifty live scorpions? Well, the answer is to pro-test Tuna's upcoming Varmint, Critter and Pest Fest, now only two weeks away. All kinds of food and iced tea will be served, and there will be demonstrations on how to kill fire ants, killer bees, scorpions, tarantulas, bats and all four venomous snakes that reside within our city limits. Do you remember the time that taran-tula climbed out of the church organ while Cooter Wooten was playing "When the Role Is Called up Yonder?"

ARLES. That's when she picked up that stammer.

THURSTON. She did.

ARLES. She did, she did.

(**ARLES** *exits and changes to* **DIDI SNAVELY**.)

THURSTON. She's never been the same. Now folks, it's time for a word from our regular sponsor here on Radio Station OKKK, and here she is herself, Didi Snavely of Didi's Used Weapons. Didi.

(**DIDI** *enters.*)

DIDI. This is Didi Snavely reminding you on this national holiday that fireworks make a pop, but a good fire-arm makes a point. Now, when our nation's founders won their independence from the ugly English, they didn't win it by inviting' them over for tea and crum-pets. They won it because they shot 'em. And the English were obviously slow learners because they came back over here in 1812 and they shot 'em again. And they shot the Spanish at the turn of the century, too. I don't remember why, but you know they had it coming. This country's freedom wasn't purchased with peace marches, protests, and EST seminars. We bought it with bullets, bombs, and bayonets. So come down to the store, demonstrate your commitment to the Second Amendment, and never forget that if our Texas forefathers had had bigger and better weaponry, it would be Mexico that remembers the Alamo.

(**DIDI** *exits and changes to* **ARLES**. **ARLES** *enters during below.*))

THURSTON. Thank you, Didi, thank you. Well folks, it's always a pleasure to have Didi here with us. This just in. We just got word that Joe Bob Lipsey has walked out of final rehearsals for his Fourth-of-July extravaganza after a squabble with the local chapter of the Smut Snatchers of the New Order. It seems the Smut Snatchers have objected to the song "I Get No Kick From Champagne" because it's being performed in a dry county, and they say if you can't drink it here, you shouldn't be able to sing about it either. Joe Bob hurled his box lunch at the Smut Snatchers present and told them to take the show and stick it up their hymnals. I'm not sure what that means.

ARLES. Well, you never know with Joe Bob.

THURSTON. You don't. At last report, Joe Bob was headed to Didi Snavely's to buy a suicide weapon.

ARLES. Well, we've all heard that before.

THURSTON. We have.

ARLES. We have, we have. Thurston, how about that weather?

THURSTON. Well, in the weather, it's gonna be hot today, slightly hotter than yesterday, and a little bit hotter tomorrow, with temperatures in the low one hundreds, but with the heat index it will feel like a hundred and twenty. I'd like to know who came up with that heat index thing.

ARLES. I could have gotten by just fine without that information. And from our world news desk, death toll rises as Muslims fight Hindus at Buddhist holy shrine. Looks like those folks could learn to act like Christians.

THURSTON. It does.

ARLES. It does, it does.

THURSTON. This is Thurston Wheelis.

ARLES. And this is Arles Struvie, saying Happy Independence Day.

(Lights fade. Music. **ARLES** *exits and changes to* **PETEY FISK.** **THURSTON** *exits and changes to* **BERTHA BUMILLER.** *Lights come up as* **PETEY** *enters.)*

PETEY. This is Petey Fisk speaking to you for the Greater Tuna Humane Society, and I'd like to encourage all listeners to boycott the upcoming Varmint, Critter and Pest Fest. Now the word "pest" does not merely apply to creatures that buzz, bite or climb the wall on more than one set of appendages. It also refers to jerks on jet skis, lumps with leaf blowers, and anybody who leaves their beeper or cell phone on in the theatre. So-called pests suffer greatly at the hands of enlightened society. So think about it. And remember that mosquitoes have a life expectancy of one week, that centipedes are always on their feet, and that rattlesnakes, unlike humans, warn you before attempting to take your life. This is Petey Fisk speaking to you for the Greater Tuna Humane Society. Thank you.

*(***PETEY*** exits.)*

Scene Three

(Lights come up to reveal the interior of **BERTHA BUMILLER***'s kitchen and living room. "Misty"* comes up, and* **BERTHA BUMILLER** *enters. She makes herself busy about the house, the doorbell rings and she turns the radio off.* **PETEY** *appears at* **BERTHA***'s screen door.)*

PETEY. Hey, Bertha.

*(***PETEY** *enters through the imaginary screen door.)*

BERTHA. Happy 4th of July, Petey.

PETEY. I wanted to pay my condolences. I'm so sorry you had to put Woofie down.

BERTHA. I appreciate that, Petey. We waited as long as we could, hoping she would come around. But she was blind, deaf, and down to one good leg.

PETEY. Lord, that's worse than Didi Snavely's mother.

BERTHA. Almost.

PETEY. It must have been tough at the vet.

BERTHA. Well, yes and no. We took her to Lubbock to Dr. Fites and Woofie was so far gone she didn't even try to bite him.

PETEY. Well, she was ready to go.

BERTHA. Oh yes. We buried her behind that holly bush but Shep dug her up and slung her all over the yard.

PETEY. That's a bird dog for you. *(pause)* So you're down to only six dogs.

BERTHA. What are you getting at?

PETEY. Well, I just thought...

BERTHA. Don't even start. Oh God, did you bring that box with you?

PETEY. Box?

BERTHA. On the porch.

PETEY. Well.

BERTHA. You've got a dog in that box.

PETEY. No, I don't.

*See Music Note on page 3

BERTHA. Don't lie to me.

PETEY. I'm not.

BERTHA. I wasn't born in a blue state. Get that dog out of here.

PETEY. It's not a dog exactly.

BERTHA. Well, what exactly is it.

PETEY. Well, it started out as a cat.

BERTHA. You're talking like a spook.

PETEY. Let me finish. This little kitten turned up behind a liquor store in Lubbock and a friend brought him to me when he was three days old. His name is Pinkey.

BERTHA. I'm not taking a cat.

PETEY. He's not exactly a cat. Well, when Pinkey arrived I had this neurotic little Pomeranian named Cassie who had to be forced to nurse her own puppies. But mean as she was, she had a soft spot for Pinkey right off the bat and gave him all the milk he wanted. He became her favorite and turned out just like her.

BERTHA. What do you mean?

PETEY. He thinks he's a dog.

BERTHA. Shut up.

PETEY. He does. He bites tires, chews up slippers and guards the yard.

BERTHA. I don't believe that.

PETEY. I'm telling you, he's an attack cat. He'll keep the Amway salesmen beyond the gate, I'll tell you that.

BERTHA. You must think I'm crazy...

PETEY. Look Bertha, there's a couple of Jehovah Witnesses at the back gate right now.

BERTHA. Oh, God, nothing makes me madder than a so-called Christian that doesn't believe in war. Let it out of the box.

(**PETEY** *steps outside and after a moment the sound of a hostile cat is heard.* **PETEY** *steps back in.*)

BERTHA. Well, would you look at them leap that fence. I'll take the cat. What does he eat?

PETEY. Any good dry dog food.

BERTHA. Don't worry; he'll have a good home here. Hey, Pinkey, stop digging in my flowerbed. Oh, look at him lifting his leg. He's so cute...

PETEY. *(as he exits)* And if you want to take him out of the yard, I've left his leash in the box. Bye, Bertha.

*(**PETEY** exits and changes into **CHARLENE BUMILLER**.)*

BERTHA. Bye, Petey.

*(**BERTHA** turns on the radio.)*

VOICE OF ARLES. That was our song, and the first of many, going out to my dearest baby, Bertha, on the eve of our wedding. This just in to the OKKK news room: Local militia leader Elmer Watkins and three followers have just taken Reba Childers hostage in her own home and they say they will not release her until the state government recognizes the northeast corner of Dewey County as the free and independent nation of Free White Texas.

VOICE OF THURSTON. *(on the radio)* What?

VOICE OF ARLES. *(on the radio)* Reba, well known wilderness scout and wife of local mayor Leonard Childers, has requested that everybody stay away and says she can handle the situation by herself.

VOICE OF THURSTON. *(on the radio)* You got that right. She knows eight kinds of martial arts.

VOICE OF ARLES. *(on the radio)* She could bring down an elephant with an emery board.

VOICE OF THURSTON. *(on the radio)* She could do it on a sick day. The woman's deadly.

*(**CHARLENE** enters.)*

VOICE OF ARLES. *(on the radio)* She is.

VOICE OF THURSTON. *(on the radio)* She is.

VOICE OF ARLES. *(on the radio)* She is. She is. We'll have more on this breaking story as it develops.

*(**BERTHA** turns the radio off.)*

BERTHA. Charlene, honey, what would you like for breakfast?

CHARLENE. Oh, I can't think of food at a time like this. All I can think about is Rayford.

BERTHA. Well, you need to think about somebody a little closer. You wanted to be an army wife, Rayford's overseas, and you knew he was going to be when you married him.

CHARLENE. I guess that's my lot in life, to be trapped here in Dog Patch while he's off defending our country in some hostile outpost.

BERTHA. He's cooking hamburgers in Guam, Charlene. The worst thing that could happen to him is a grill burn. Have you tried on your new maternity dress for the wedding?

CHARLENE. I hate it. You know I can't stand anything that shade of blue.

BERTHA. You have to wear it for good luck. You're the something-blue in the wedding.

CHARLENE. What's the something-old? Arles?

BERTHA. You are so hateful on an empty stomach.

CHARLENE. That's right, pick on me. You've got one child who spray paints road-kill.

BERTHA. Stanley makes very good money with his artwork.

CHARLENE. And another child who goes to South America to look for bugs.

BERTHA. You should be very proud of Jody for getting that biology scholarship.

CHARLENE. Well, if he sends one more cockroach home in the mail, I'm calling the cops. That last one nearly put me in false labour. It's just like you to defend those two while I have to have my baby here alone.

BERTHA. What is this "alone" business? What am I, Velveeta?

CHARLENE. I wouldn't expect you to understand.

BERTHA. I understand that you better eat. Pregnant women need nourishment.

CHARLENE. All right. I'll have some yogurt, but only for the baby.

(*CHARLENE moves to the refrigerator and opens it.*)

BERTHA. Charlene, are you going to the class reunion today?

CHARLENE. Oh, I don't think so. I hated high school. All I see is half-and-half. Don't we have any heavy cream?

BERTHA. It's behind the Spam.

CHARLENE. Thank God. No, they'll just have to have their reunion without me. I'll come back in another ten years after Rayford and I have moved to California. Don't tell me we're out of candied fruit.

BERTHA. It's right in front of you. And what is this about you and Rayford moving to California?

CHARLENE. We are, as soon as he gets out the Army. We're moving to Bakersfield. I hear it's like paradise. Do we have any real sugar?

BERTHA. It's in the canister marked "Sugar." Why do you want to move to Bakersfield?

CHARLENE. It's our natural spirit of adventure. You don't think I'm gonna sit around here with nothing better to do than burp the Tupperware.

BERTHA. You'll think burp when that baby is born.

CHARLENE. I'll make a great Army wife, just like Jessica Lange in that movie.

BERTHA. She went nuts in that movie, Charlene.

CHARLENE. Well, then, just like Donna Reed in *From Here To Eternity.*

BERTHA. She went nuts, too.

CHARLENE. Well, then, just like Jane Fonda in that movie about Viet Nam.

BERTHA. She married a man in a wheelchair, Charlene. You couldn't push a wheelchair ten feet without stopping for a Coke.

CHARLENE. Where are the malted milk balls?

BERTHA. Stanley ate them when he came in last night.

CHARLENE. All of them?

BERTHA. I guess so. There weren't that many.

CHARLENE. *(starts to cry)* I can see nobody gives a fig about my baby's nutrition.

BERTHA. What?

CHARLENE. I can't take much more. Rayford hasn't called in three days, my feet are swelling, the doctor won't let me eat salt, and now no malted milk balls. *(She exits, crying.)*

BERTHA. Charlene, honey, where are you going?

CHARLENE. *(crying)* Back to bed.

  *(**CHARLENE** exits and changes to **STANLEY BUMILLER**.)*

BERTHA. *(yells after her)* Honey, I've got half a Butterfinger out in the car.

  *(**BERTHA** turns on the radio in time to hear the last word of a Patsy Cline song.)*

  Shoot, I missed it.

VOICE OF ARLES. *(on the radio)* That was for you, my dearest baby, on the eve of our wedding. And folks, in the local-boy-does-good department, Stanley Bumiller, who is soon to be my stepson, and who was voted 'Most Likely to Succumb' by his senior class, has returned for his mother's wedding to yours-truly in a hail of glory. Can you believe it folks, he has clean hair, lots of money, and is considered the demigod of the Southwestern art world with his neo-taxidermy spray-paint creations. And Stanley has done an art piece as a gift to the citizens of Tuna, which will be unveiled at the dedication ceremony later today for the newly named Buckner High School here in Tuna.

VOICE OF THURSTON. And to think, Stanley had once been sent to reform school by Judge Buckner. It's ironic.

VOICE OF ARLES. It is.

VOICE OF THURSTON. It is.

VOICE OF ARLES. It is, it is.

(**STANLEY** *enters and turns the radio off.*)

BERTHA. Good morning, Honey. What would you like for breakfast?

STANLEY. *(moves to the coffee pot and pours a cup)* Do we have any of those malted milk balls?

BERTHA. No, you ate them all last night. And don't mention it around Charlene, or she'll have a fit. It's hard to believe she's going to have a baby.

STANLEY. You got that right. Think of her husband. That couldn't have been easy.

BERTHA. Behave. Now, I want you to take her with you to the high school reunion.

STANLEY. I'm not going.

BERTHA. Don't you want to see all your old friends?

STANLEY. Yeah, all my old friends who wouldn't have squat to do with me when I got out of reform school.

BERTHA. They were just being kids, honey. Besides, you have to be there when they unveil your art; that's all there is to it.

STANLEY. I'm not going, and I couldn't take Charlene if I was.

BERTHA. Why?

STANLEY. She's too big to fit in my sports car.

BERTHA. You will act like a Christian to your sister, or I'll slap the snot out of you. She's not that big. We got her into the back seat of a Volkswagen just last week.

STANLEY. No.

BERTHA. I just think you'd have a good time at the reunion, that's all. And you have to go vote for your Aunt Pearl. Helen and Inita are serving her prize-winning potato salad and I know how much you like that.

STANLEY. I do love that potato salad.

BERTHA. It's so good of you to create a work of art for your home town.

STANLEY. Yeah, I've always wanted to give something back to Tuna, Texas.

BERTHA. I'm so proud of your success with your art, but honey I don't understand it.

STANLEY. It's simple, really. Now the animals exist as symbols of nature's fragile existence in a world dehumanised by the mechanical symbiosis of those being hurtled through time and terra nova towards an uncertain destiny, which may or may not exist depending on the random and coincidental happenstances that unite man and nature in an apex of destruction and I spray paint them because the colors are pretty.

BERTHA. But, Stanley, what does all that mean?

STANLEY. It means folks in Santa Fe will pay out the butt for 'em.

BERTHA. I never cared much for Santa Fe. Your daddy and I stopped there on the way to Pike's Peak and had lunch, and all the waiters had diapers wrapped around their heads. They looked like Q-tips.

STANLEY. They were seiks.

BERTHA. I'll say they were.

STANLEY. Momma.

BERTHA. And when your daddy found out they didn't serve meat, he got so mad he jumped in the car and drove straight for Texas. He never stopped again until he found a chicken-fried steak.

STANLEY. Remember the time we all went to Sea World, and Daddy threw a fit because the killer whales didn't kill anything?

BERTHA. He sure was disappointed.

STANLEY. So, where are you and Arles going to go on your honeymoon?

BERTHA. Well, Arles wants to go to Sweetwater to the Rattlesnake Roundup, but I'm determined to go to Eureka Springs, Arkansas, to the Passion Play.

STANLEY. Boy.

BERTHA. You can come with us if you want to.

STANLEY. No, I've got to get back to Santa Fe. I've got fifty animals to spray-paint and frame by Friday week. I'd appreciate it if you'd do me a favour, though.

BERTHA. What?

STANLEY. Could you get Arles to quit calling you Baby? Now, don't get me wrong, I like Arles, but I can't stand it when he calls you Baby. It just makes me...*(at a loss for words)*

BERTHA. Well, I am his baby, Baby.

STANLEY. Mama, you are too old and too...*(searches for the word)* ...stout to be called Baby.

BERTHA. *(getting mad)* Stanley, I'll have you know I feel all warm inside when he calls me Baby, just like one of your Aunt Pearl's hot apple turnovers.

STANLEY. Hey, I can't take that kind of talk.

BERTHA. Stanley, you need to wake up and smell the Sanka.

STANLEY. I'm sorry, Mama. I should have kept my mouth shut. I mean, it's not like you're going on a real honeymoon, or you wouldn't have invited me.

BERTHA. Of course we're going on a real honeymoon. What are you driving at?

STANLEY. Well, you know.

BERTHA. I'm sure I don't. *(pause)* Are you going to tell me, or do I call the Psychic Friends Network?

STANLEY. *(obviously having a hard time with the subject)* I just mean, it's not like you're going to stay in the same room or sleep in the same bed or anything.

BERTHA. Well of course we are.

STANLEY. *(shocked beyond belief)* Mama!

BERTHA. Well, where did you think we were going to sleep, one in the room and the other in the car?

STANLEY. *(stunned)* Mama, you ought to be ashamed of yourself. You're too old to act like that.

BERTHA. Stanley Gene, what did you think we were going to do on our honeymoon, play Yahtzee and cook s'mores?

STANLEY. Oh, I can't hear this. *(starts to exit)*

BERTHA. Stanley, sex is the foundation of any good marriage.

STANLEY. I can't hear this. First you let him call you Baby, and now this. Hell, I gotta go.

(STANLEY exits through screen door and changes to VERA CARP.)

BERTHA. *(yells after him)* Stanley, you need to get out more. You spend too much time around those dead animals. You need to get out in the world and mix. *(to herself)* Oh well, he just needs somebody to call him Baby. *(She looks at her watch.)* I hope Arles remembers to play some Tammy Wynette for me. *(She moves to turn on the radio, but the telephone rings before she gets to it.)* Shoot.

(BERTHA answers the phone. VERA enters to other side of stage and sits.)

Hello.

VERA. Bertha?

BERTHA. Hello, Vera.

VERA. Bertha, Bertha, don't you think you might want to reconsider wearing white to the wedding tomorrow?

BERTHA. Vera, I don't have any problem getting remarried in white. It's not like we're both divorced. You know that Hank dropped dead when he found me dancing with Arles at the Christmas Eve party.

VERA. Yes, but don't you think you might want to go with a beige, or sort of a bone-white? I mean, you are marrying a divorced man, and in my house no less.

BERTHA. Yes, it's so nice of you to insist on the wedding being at your house.

VERA. No problem. Your family is my family, within reason. But I would appreciate it if you would keep them away until I get all the furniture covered with plastic. Hang on. *(calls off)* Lupe, Lupe, *(in Spanish)* attencion. Lupe, when you finish covering that furniture with plastic, I want you to get right back to that picture window and clean it till it squeaks. Squeaks. Squeaks. You know, squeak, squeak, squeak. *(back into the phone)* She just looked at me like I was crazy.

BERTHA. Vera, I thought Lupe quit working for you.

VERA. Oh, she did. I decided to call all my maids Lupe. I don't have time to learn a new name every time the Border Patrol gets lucky. And I tell you, I've been as dizzy as a schizophrenic on a tilt-a-whirl about that reunion queen contest. Thank God for all of us I won. It sure would have saved us all a load of time and money if Didi and Pearl had come to their senses before now. I mean, Didi is nice, considering her background, but nobody's gonna vote for a woman who wears nothing but plastic.

BERTHA. She wears plastic because it's easy to clean. Now, Vera, you know I like Didi.

VERA. Well, that's so Christian of you.

BERTHA. I'm sure you'd have won no matter what, Vera.

VERA. I don't know. It was a secret ballot. I hate the whole concept of secret ballots, it's so sneaky. And I'm sure Pearl would have raked up a few sympathy votes, the poor thing, but can you picture her trying to wear a tiara? Good Lord, she'd have to use scotch tape to keep it on.

BERTHA. Vera, that's so mean.

VERA. I didn't invent the truth. You have to have hair to wear a tiara. I went to college in Fort Worth; I know what I'm talking about. Hang on. *(calls off)* Virgil! Virgil, you put those car keys back in my purse right this instant. I don't even want you looking toward the garage. You are still grounded.

BERTHA. Vera, why is Virgil grounded this time?

VERA. Oh, I can't remember. I'd have to look it up.

BERTHA. He must be happy to be home from military school.

VERA. You know, I am so disappointed in that place. Virgil's commanding officer had fought in half a dozen wars, so we thought he could instill some discipline,

VERA. *(cont.)* but after six months with Virgil, he quit the Army and got a job selling tweezers. Why did we have kids in the first place?

BERTHA. Sometimes I wonder. I pray Charlene's water doesn't break anytime soon.

VERA. Oh, she sure is getting big. I'd keep her on linoleum if I were you. Hang on. *(calls off)* Virgil, don't shake that lava lamp. It's an antique. I mean it. I'll come over there and shake you. Young man, if you want your driving privileges restored, you had better brighten the corner where you are. *(into the phone)* Well, I'm just barely prepared for that Smut Snatchers' meeting this afternoon. Reverend Spikes is going to be there, and you know how high strung he can be when he first gets out of prison.

BERTHA. Does he still take off running when he hears a police siren?

VERA. Yes. It'd be funny if it wasn't so sad. And I've been so busy rewriting all those Bible school songs to root out any vestiges of secular humanism.

BERTHA. You've been working very hard, Vera.

VERA. Tell me. I haven't had time to read a lick. I hardly feel Christian if I can't find at least one book a week that needs to be banned.

BERTHA. Vera, Arles gave me a copy of "Lonesome Dove" and I can't find anything wrong with it.

VERA. Well I can.

BERTHA. What?

VERA. Well, they use the word "poke" every ten seconds.

BERTHA. I say poke all the time.

VERA. Well, stop.

BERTHA. Vera, I used to poke Hank in church to keep him awake.

VERA. Oh my Lord. I hope nobody is picking this up on their cell phones. Back to my earlier point, have you and Arles decided on a minister for the wedding?

BERTHA. Arles wants to use his cousin Slim for the service, Vera. He's an ordained Methodist minister.

VERA. Methodist? You can't get married by a Methodist. They don't believe in baptism.

BERTHA. Yes they do. They just sprinkle instead of dunk.

VERA. Well, if that's all the water they're going to use, why don't they do it with a squirt gun? Hang on. *(calls off)* Lupe, Darlin', you forgot to cover that footstool with plastic. Foot stool....*(VERA shakes her foot.)* Foot stool... Oh my Lord, I got her dancing. Alto, Lupe, alto! I'll get drummed out of the Smut Snatchers if my Baptist friends catch me with a dancing maid. Let me call you back.

(VERA exits and changes to STANLEY. BERTHA takes out a piece of paper and writes a note to ARLES.)

BERTHA. Dear Arles. No. *(She wads up paper.)* Dearest Arles, *(Stops, wads another sheet, writes.)* Dear Blue Racer, you'll have to be quicker than your old blue racer to catch me this morning. I have a million things to do and you are not on time. You can find me at Didi's. *(stops writing, to herself)* Boy, she's been loading her guns over this Vera thing, and Aunt Pearl is up to something, too! I don't trust them! Stanley got in last night and woke up acting like a nun. Charlene's watching "Giant" and won't get up and answer the door. If Jody sends another bug in the mail she probably will break her water. *(writing)* Are you sure you know what you're getting into marrying into this family? Ha. Ha. If you miss me at Didi's we'll meet up at the reunion near the yearbook table. Love...Slowpoke. P.S. Beware of the cat.

(BERTHA gets up and gets her purse and goes to the screen door to pin on the note. We hear the last "Look at me" of "Misty." BERTHA exits and changes to PEARL. "Misty" plays to end.)*

*See MUSIC USE NOTE on page 3

Scene Four

(Lights crossfade to Pearl's Boudoir. We hear **STANLEY** *calling from off.)*

STANLEY. *(off)* Pearl. *(pause, off still, but closer)* Pearl, are you here? *(pause)*

*(***STANLEY** *enters Pearl's Boudoir and looks around he peeks into the adjoining room.)*

Uncle Henry, it's me, Stanley. Where's Aunt Pearl?

(We hear **PEARL** *off.)*

PEARL. *(offstage)* Stanley, is that you? Where are you?

*(***PEARL** *enters from another part of the house.)*

STANLEY. I'm looking for you.

PEARL. Honey, don't wake up your Uncle Henry; he'll be no good tonight. Let me look at you; you've gotten so handsome. I've been meaning to call you. I want you to escort me to the reunion this afternoon.

*(***PEARL** *sits at her imaginary dresser to apply makeup and talks to* **STANLEY,** *at times to his reflection in the dresser's mirror on the fourth wall.)*

STANLEY. I'm not dressed for the reunion, Pearl. I just stopped by to say 'hi' before all the wedding ruckus tomorrow, 'cause soon as that's over, I'm out of here.

PEARL. Stanley, something's wrong. What is it, honey? Aren't you happy for your mother?

STANLEY. Yeah, I guess.

PEARL. Then tell me what's wrong.

STANLEY. Oh, nothing.

PEARL. Well, you should be dancing on the clouds, coming home a success. Who'd have ever thought you would one day be dedicating a piece of your sculpture in honor of that awful judge that sent you to reform school? And it's so good of you to donate it to your hometown, although they don't deserve it. Tell me what it looks like.

STANLEY. I don't want to ruin the surprise, Pearl.

PEARL. You get your talent from my side of the family. Why, one time in school, I made a whole set of farm animals out of corn flakes, rice and dried beans.

STANLEY. Really? You still got them?

PEARL. Oh, no. We ate them during the Depression. Stanley, what's wrong with you? Why are you so melancholy? You're not still holding a grudge against Judge Buchner, are you, Stanley? You've got to move on.

STANLEY. I'm sorry, Pearl. You're right.

PEARL. Your momma and Arles are so lucky. It's the best time to get married, when you're too old to have kids. They're going to have a wonderful time.

STANLEY. You've got that right. Mama's flouncing around like Salome. I find that real hard to take.

PEARL. Find what hard to take?

STANLEY. You know. Mama…and Arles… *(softly)*…and sex.

PEARL. Oh, it's them having sex that's bothering you. Well relax, honey, that's just part of life.

STANLEY. At their age?

PEARL. Oh, it only gets better. I wouldn't give you day old bread for my sex life before I turned sixty-five.

STANLEY. Oh no, Pearl, not you, too.

PEARL. Well, Honey. Aren't you getting any?

STANLEY. Oh, please.

PEARL. That's why my first marriage to your uncle Henry came apart and ended in divorce. Forty-seven years of the same-o, same-o. And what do you think retired folks do with all that time on their hands?

STANLEY. You're killing me!

PEARL. Your Aunt Ruby had to move out of the rest home because of all that carousing going on. She couldn't get a wink of sleep.

STANLEY. Why are you telling me this? I have to go home and take a shower.

PEARL. Honey, wait; let me get you a glass of iced tea.

STANLEY. No. The heat will bring me to. Goodbye, Pearl.

(**STANLEY** *exits and changes to* **DIDI**.)

PEARL. Goodbye, honey. Oh, Stanley, poor darling. Who would have dreamed you'd grow up to be a nun.

(**PEARL** *exits toward the adjoining room and changes to* **JOE BOB**.)

Scene Five

(Lights change to Didi's Used Weapons Shop. **DIDI** *sings "The Battle of New Orleans" from offstage. She pauses from time to time to inhale her cigarette, continues the lyrics in her head, and picks up singing aloud with the exhale. She enters, continuing to sing and smoke. She takes another drag, notices something that upsets her and calls offstage.)*

DIDI. Mama, Mama, don't put those bunny rabbit slippers in the radar range. That's not a rabbit hutch, Mama, it's a microwave oven. Don't push that button. God... *(The microwave dings.)*...damn it. Well, we'll be tasting that for a week. Mama, get out your bingo cards from under the bed. That'll slow her down long enough for me to have a smoke.

(A cowbell rings and **JOE BOB LIPSEY** *enters, striking a dramatic pose at the door.)*

Hello, Joe Bob, how are you?

JOE BOB. I've had it. I've had it, I've had it, I've had it.

DIDI. Well, I'm glad somebody's had it.

JOE BOB. I've had it with this tiny little town with its tiny little minds. How dare Vera Carp say I can't have reference to champagne in a dry county? She wouldn't know champagne from brake fluid.

DIDI. Don't get me going on her. That woman needs a good killing. I miss the old days when you can go to the wrong side of Houston with fifty dollars and get anybody in the state killed before sundown. We lost something when that went away.

JOE BOB. That reminds me. I need a suicide weapon. I'm gonna end it all and become a martyr for my art.

DIDI. I wish I could help you, Joe Bob, but I've got a long standing policy about selling guns to suicidal customers. It's cost me a fortune at tax time.

JOE BOB. Rules are meant to be broken. I just want to die.

DIDI. Now, I've never been against the principal that people have the right to shoot each other. If they couldn't could you imagine the chaos?

JOE BOB. Didi, you've known me since I was in diapers.

DIDI. Oh.

JOE BOB. Can't you make an exception?

DIDI. Suicide is in direct conflict with God's law, and I think anyone who gets caught trying should get the death penalty.

JOE BOB. Where in the Bible does it talk about suicide?

DIDI. It's in there. Mama can find it. *(She calls off, then gets up and goes off.)* Mama, Mama, quit playing bingo for a minute. I want you to get out your bible and look up what it says about taking your own life....taking your own life. No, Mama, nobody's going to take away your knife. Get out from under the table. God.....dammit! B-26! That's better. *(She re-enters.)* I got her playing imaginary bingo. It's the only way to keep her calm.

JOE BOB. You know, Didi, I hoped you'd show a little compassion and spring for a spoonful of poison after all the money the little theatre spent here on props for "Annie Get Your Gun."

DIDI. And you got peanut butter all over my best squirrel rifle. I can't even give it away.

JOE BOB. Peanut Butter? That must have been when I was on that health kick.

DIDI. But back to getting killed, you don't have to stoop to suicide. Not around here. You want to die, have someone do it for you. Scratch on a bathroom window, pin on a Bill Clinton button, or blow a kiss at the wrong cowboy. If you can't get yourself killed in a small town in Texas, you're not really trying.

JOE BOB. Maybe I'll just starve myself to death.

DIDI. That's gonna take a while.

JOE BOB. I came here wanting to kill myself, seeking a little support from you, and wind up with bupkis. Didi, you're really bringing me down.

DIDI. Joe Bob, you need to get out your Norman Vincent Peale. Just because people laugh at you behind your back and you don't have a love life, and you dress funny, and you haven't had a hit since "L'il Abner," doesn't mean things can't get better.

JOE BOB. May I remind you that "Oklahoma" was a monster hit?

DIDI. I missed that one. R.R.'s family is from Stillwater. I'll be damned if I'm going to sit through a musical about a place like that. But back to my point, things can get better. Look at me. In the last few years, my sister's husband got sent to Alaska so we can't afford to call much less visit. Mama's gotten so senile all she can do is play imaginary bingo, and my husband's disappeared off the face of the earth. If all those blessings can fall on me, why not you.

JOE BOB. *(looking out the window)* I've got to go, Didi. Helen's and Inita's food booth just opened up. I better get in line. If this is to be my last meal, I need to get there before they run out of potato salad. It's been nice knowing you, Didi.

DIDI. If that depression gets worse, feel free to call me anytime. Well, not during Jerry Springer. Bye, Joe Bob.

(JOE BOB exits – cowbell rings – and changes to PEARL. DIDI turns on radio.)

VOICE OF THURSTON. *(on the radio)* This is Thurston Wheelis with a news update. Reba Childers just called the station to say that she has disarmed and tied up all three militia leaders who invaded her home earlier today. She has a message for the other members of the group known as Free White Texas. She says the militia members tracked mud all over her rugs, and if she doesn't receive four hundred dollars by 5:30 p.m. she's going to kill all three of them. And she won't take checks. We'll have more on the situation as it develops.

(The cowbell rings on DIDI's door, PEARL enters.)

DIDI. Come on in, Pearl, I've been expecting you.

PEARL. Oh, I'm so mad at that Vera Carp my nose hairs hurt.

DIDI. Vera can do that to you.

PEARL. Telling all those lies about my chickens spreading bird flu.

DIDI. And blaming me for R.R.'s drinking when everybody knows I'm nothing if not a moderating influence. And claiming R.R. abandoned me when we all know he just disappeared. One more day and he's legally dead.

PEARL. And the gall of Vera to offer us a place on the float at her feet. Those big old ugly hooves.

DIDI. I've seen rowboats that were smaller.

PEARL. They oughta come with an anchor. Now, Didi, I want you to cover me and I'm gonna put marbles in her hubcaps.

DIDI. I've got a better idea.

PEARL. Lets' pour rock salt in her flowerbeds and see how those peach colored gladiolas hold up.

DIDI. That's kid stuff.

PEARL. I'll call in a bomb threat to her husband's bank.

DIDI. That's been done to death. You gotta think big.

PEARL. Like what?

DIDI. Let's kill her. I'll provide the gun at cost and you can do the hit. Even if you get caught you're too old to go to prison.

PEARL. You really think so?

DIDI. You'd be doing us all a favor.

PEARL. Oh, I could bring her down like a top heavy pheasant.

DIDI. I'd say let Mama do it, but she's so far gone there's no telling who she might shoot. Last week she took her walker out, waddled up to the Tastee Kreme, and left her gun lying right there on the coffee table.

PEARL. Oh, that's not like her. She's losing her grip.

DIDI. Just treadin' water.

PEARL. Oh, Didi, it just hit me. I can't shoot Vera. I promised Henry I'd never use a firearm again. It's the only way he would remarry me.

DIDI. That was awful all that red tape you went through when you shot that second husband.

PEARL. Don't ever marry a sleep walker.

DIDI. If R.R. had been one I'd have left the door open years ago.

PEARL. Oh, I was thinking about R.R. just the other day. I read about a U.F.O. in the National Inquisitor. It said a U.F.O. came down and picked a man up in Arkansas three years ago and then brought him back last month to get his suspenders. Well, here's the scary part. It said that he could just snap his fingers and you couldn't make a sound. That your lips would move and nothing would come out. Just by snapping his fingers he made a whole town in Arkansas shut up. Can you imagine anyone in Arkansas shuttin' up?

DIDI. You don't believe that, do you, Pearl?

PEARL. What?

DIDI. You don't believe what you read in those magazines.

PEARL. Oh, they wouldn't print it if it weren't true.

DIDI. But back to Vera, maybe we should run a write-in candidate.

PEARL. Is that legal?

DIDI. Oh, it goes all the way back to the Bible.

PEARL. Really?

DIDI. Oh, Mama can find it. *(She yells off.)* Mama...Mama... Look up in the Bible where it talks about write-in elections. Elections. Elections. No, Mama, you don't have an infection. God...dammit, don't start that again. I'll be right back, Pearl. She's likely to eat another Alka Seltzer. I don't want her foaming like a mad dog. *(exiting)* Just one more thing for me to clean up. If I don't stop her she'll eat every baby aspirin in the house.

*(**DIDI** exits and changes to **ARLES**.)*

PEARL. I'm going to run on, Didi. I've got to get back and feed Henry. *(PEARL looks at an imaginary thermometer. To herself)* What does that thermometer say? Lord, it's a hundred degrees. I hope my rooster can hold up in this heat. Why our forefathers declared independence on the hottest day of the year is a mystery to me. Looks like they could have waited till autumn.

(The cowbell rings as PEARL exits and changes to BERTHA. We hear DIDI offstage.)

DIDI *(offstage)* Momma, Momma, we've been through this before. You can't smoke for thirty minutes if you've had ammunition in your mouth. N-48. N-48.

MOMMA *(offstage)* Bingo!

DIDI *(offstage)* Don't dump your card till you double check your numbers. No, Mama, No. Put the paint ball gun down. I can't believe I left that sitting out. You already ruined my new Aztec calendar. I can't have nothing nice.

(The cowbell rings and ARLES enters.)

ARLES. Didi, Didi, are you here?

(The cowbell rings and BERTHA enters.)

Hey, baby.

BERTHA. Arles, you got my note.

ARLES. It's nice and cool in here. I tell you I'm hotter than a pregnant mouse in a wool sock. *(He kisses her cheek and sniffs the air.)* Oh, you've done it again.

BERTHA. Done what?

ARLES. Give me another whiff.

BERTHA. Oh, my perfume. I forgot what affect Omaha Nights has on you.

ARLES. Don't you put it on again till after the wedding. A man can only take so much temptation.

BERTHA. Stop. Didi's made some ice tea. You want some.

ARLES. Is it that instant with artificial lemon in it?

BERTHA. It sure is.

ARLES. I can't say no. I'm gonna stand over here by the air conditioner.

BERTHA. I tell you, Arles, if I had it to do over again, I would elope.

ARLES. I hear you, Baby.

BERTHA. Vera is about to drive me crazy with all these details. You know how she can be.

ARLES. Well, you know, I've always liked Vera, but not very much.

BERTHA. Well, she's about to have a fit because I'm enjoying "Lonesome Dove." I guess I'm going to have to read some more of the books we've banned. There's no telling what I've missed.

ARLES. That's the spirit.

BERTHA. Arles, you're so good for me. I enjoy life so much more with you in the picture. Here's your tea.

ARLES. Thank you, Baby. *(They drink.)* God bless whoever came up with instant tea.

BERTHA. I like it too.

ARLES. I got 'em.

BERTHA. Got what?

ARLES. Forty-eight hour passes to the Rattlesnake Roundup.

BERTHA. Oh.

ARLES. Something wrong, Baby?

BERTHA. Well, I've been meaning to bring that up, Arles. I really don't want to go there for our honeymoon.

ARLES. Why not?

BERTHA. Well, it's not very romantic, for one thing.

ARLES. Oh, you're going to love it.

BERTHA. Oh, Arles, let's go to Eureka Springs, Arkansas to the Passion Play. I've always wanted to.

ARLES. Talk about unromantic; that's not the kind of passion I had in mind.

BERTHA. Oh, it'll be great. We'll be up there in those cool mountains, and they say the play is wonderful. They have a new Jesus this year. He's a student from Texas A&M. Vera said he sent shivers down her spine.

ARLES. Baby, my mama dragged me to Sunday school for eighteen straight years. There's nothing you can tell me about Jesus.

BERTHA. Arles!

ARLES. Now, I'm bound and determined to have a better honeymoon than the one with Trudy. We went to Mount Saint Helens. God, what a flop that was.

BERTHA. I thought you weren't going to bring up Trudy. Well, my honeymoon wasn't any better. Hank took me to the drive-in movies in Del Rio.

ARLES. *(disgusted)* Hank. Hank. Hank.

BERTHA. The worst part was I'd already seen *I Spit on Your Grave, Part 2.* So, don't you see that's why I want to go to the Passion Play?

ARLES. Baby, I don't want to spend my honeymoon watching play-acting from the Bible.

BERTHA. Well, I don't want to have to check under my wedding bed for rattlesnakes.

ARLES. You got a stubborn streak, you know that? If everything doesn't go your way you get all huffy.

BERTHA. *(getting huffy)* When do I get all huffy?

ARLES. Well, you got all huffy over the wedding music and I gave in.

BERTHA. I am not about to walk down the aisle to the tune of "Deep in the Heart of Texas." And I didn't say a word when you insisted on wearing cowboy boots to the ceremony.

ARLES. I've worn cowboy boots every day of my life, and I'll be wearing them in the great hereafter.

BERTHA. If you make it that far.

ARLES. I'll tell you one thing, if heaven has a dress code, I'll walk to hell in my Tony Lamas.

BERTHA. I hate it when you talk like that.

ARLES. Now you sound like your friend, Vera.

BERTHA. Let's don't fight. Here, you can help me fill out my reunion form while I work on this hangnail. Read the first line.

ARLES. Name. *(He writes.)* Bertha Struvie.

BERTHA. Better write Bumiller. I don't want to jinx us before the wedding.

ARLES. I'll just put Bertha. Everyone knows who you are.

BERTHA. That's what I love about small towns.

ARLES. Yeah, it's quaint.

BERTHA. You know, Arles, you fit in here so well, moving here from a big place like Sand City.

ARLES. It took a while, but you adjust.

BERTHA. How many in your senior class?

ARLES. There was a whole pack of us. Thirty-nine.

BERTHA. Oh, I'd feel all swallowed up in a crowd that big.

ARLES. One thing I'll say for it, it sure builds your social skills.

BERTHA. What's next on there?

ARLES. Any kids. Three. Profession.

BERTHA. Put Mother. That's tougher in my book than lion taming.

ARLES. Hobbies and pets.

BERTHA. Six dogs, oh and now there's Pinkey.

ARLES. Pinkey?

BERTHA. Our new cat.

ARLES. *(alarmed)* Cat?

BERTHA. Petey Fisk brought him over today.

ARLES. Well, by God he can take it back. I hate cats.

BERTHA. You're just like my momma. She used to say cats were like Republicans. They rub up to you and purr till they get what they want and then they go pee on the couch. But it's okay, Pinkey thinks he's a dog.

ARLES. Is this air conditioner on the blink?

BERTHA. No, why?

ARLES. Because you're talking like you had a stroke

BERTHA. What?

ARLES. Well, something's wrong with your wiring if Petey Fisk has pawned a cat off on you claiming it thinks it's a dog.

BERTHA. Pinkey's stepmother was a Pomeranian. So he acts just like a dog.

ARLES. I don't care if he thinks he's a hula girl. I won't have a cat. Why, they can suck the breath right out of a baby.

BERTHA. Shut up, you sound like Charlene.

ARLES. Oh, I can assure you I do not sound like Charlene. Don't worry. I'm gonna find that cat and take him back to Petey Fisk today.

BERTHA. I don't believe I would. Pinkey is an attack cat. You reach over the fence; you'll draw back a nub.

ARLES. Are you threatening me with your cat?

BERTHA. No. I'm just trying to save you a trip to the clinic. You ought to be grateful.

ARLES. *(sarcastic)* Oh, I am. And after we get back home from the passion play, I'll make me a little pallet under the sink, and you can feed me soggy crackers every morning.

BERTHA. Are you trashing my cooking?

ARLES. No, but first you want me to go see bathrobe bible stories on my honeymoon, and now I have to watch my ass in case I'm being stalked by a rabid cat.

BERTHA. Watch your mouth.

ARLES. What?

BERTHA. Don't say ass around me, I'm a Christian.

ARLES. Ass, ass, ass, ass, ass.

BERTHA. You keep that up and you'll still be single this time tomorrow.

ARLES. Are you threatening to divorce me before we even get married?

BERTHA. What does it sound like?

ARLES. All right, by God it's off.

BERTHA. The wedding?

ARLES. I mean the whole damn outfit.

BERTHA. Well, that's fine with me. And you can wait out the rest of tornado season in your trailer house, and I hope you'll be real happy.

ARLES. And you can go to Arkansas to the Passion Play and see how an Aggie comes off as Jesus.

(ARLES exits, cowbell rings. ARLES changes to DIDI.)

BERTHA. Arles, you forgot to take your ring. Oh well, I'll just put it in the mail.

(DIDI enters.)

DIDI. Pickles, I didn't hear you come in. I was in there trying to stop Mama from chewing on my shot gun shells.

BERTHA. Did that make her sick?

DIDI. No, she's fine, but I'll have to knock that merchandise down. They've got tooth marks all over them. *(She sees BERTHA is distraught.)* What's wrong with you?

BERTHA. Promise not to tell.

DIDI. I promise.

BERTHA. It's off.

DIDI. Off?

BERTHA. The wedding. We broke off the engagement. I guess I didn't know him as well as I thought I did.

DIDI. Did he jilt you? Isn't that just like a man? Let me find you a good weapon. *(She moves to the weapons cabinet.)*

BERTHA. No, Didi. I don't need a weapon.

DIDI. I don't mean kill him. I got weapons that are designed to maim.

BERTHA. I don't want to maim him either.

DIDI. *(disappointed)* No? Now what did I do with those little exploding booby traps? They scare the hell out of whoever sets them off. I put one on the shower curtain 'cause Momma hides in there during *America's Most Wanted*, but R.R. set it off.

BERTHA. Did it scare him?

DIDI. Hell, yes. When he wanted to take a shower, he'd wait till dark and stand outside in the sprinkler.

BERTHA. Oh, Didi, I just remembered. Here I am, goin' on about Arles, and here you are about to get a divorce. Is R.R. legally dead yet?

DIDI. One more day. I've already signed up for that single-adults-only Sunday school class. I'll tell you, Pickles, I've got hormones wandering around down there with nothin' to do. Did you and Arles have another fight about the wedding music?

BERTHA. No, no. We settled that days ago. We decided on "Misty."

DIDI. Our song was "Sink the Bismark." My kind of music.

BERTHA. Funny how things change.

DIDI. Isn't it? Remember when R.R. first fell for me? How he'd follow me everywhere, wouldn't leave me alone? Back then it was infatuation. Today we'd call it stalking.

BERTHA. I loved Hank ever since that day in high school when they elected me FFA Sweetheart and he drove me all over town on that John Deere tractor. I don't know when I stopped loving him. Sometime after the twins were born. And now it looked like Arles was going to be perfect, but you know....

(The telephone rings.)

DIDI. *(has been listening and lighting a cigarette)* Damn it. Never fails. I light a cigarette, and before the smoke can hit my lungs, that damn thing rings. *(She moves to the phone.)*

BERTHA. If that's Arles, I'm not here.

(DIDI answers the phone.)

DIDI. Didi's used weapons. If we can't kill it its immortal. *(pause)* Yes, she's here, but she doesn't want to talk to you. Don't hem and haw with me. I know you've got another woman.

BERTHA. Didi.

DIDI. Let me tell you something you worthless so and so. You come in range of my rifle and I'll drop you like a flat beer. *(She hangs up.)* Pickles, I had no idea. Who is this Pinkey harlot? I know you're crying on the inside…*(phone rings)*…God dammit. Hello. Hey, I told you not to call here. You better stay away from my friend unless your ass is bullet proof.

BERTHA. I gotta go, Didi.

DIDI. Stick around, Pickles. Maybe I can figure out a way to take out Arles and Vera at the same time.

BERTHA. No, Didi, I appreciate it, I really do. I'm just going to go home and figure out what to do with all those wedding presents.

DIDI. Well, if there's any weaponry, I can always find a use for it.

BERTHA. Bye, Didi.

(**BERTHA** *exits. Cowbell rings.* **DIDI** *takes a drag. Phone rings.)*

DIDI. *(picks up phone)* Didi's used weapons. If it's not worth killing, you got the wrong number. Hello, Pearl. Uh huh. Who did you come up with to write in for Queen? Who? Say that one more time slowly. Oh, that's good thinking. Oh, Pearl, it'll kill her. Where did you learn to be so creative and mean at the same time? Well, thank God for Sunday school. I'll spread the word. See you there. And Pearl, bring some extra film. We're going to want pictures. *(She hangs up.)* Mama, I have to close up shop for a few minutes. Something's come up. Now I want you to work on your jigsaw puzzle. When you get finished we'll go to Disneyland, I promise. I hope to God she never figures out I switched a dozen pieces on her from another puzzle or we'll be trapped together forever in Fantasyland.

(**DIDI** *exits her shop – cowbell rings. Lights change to exterior.)*

DIDI. *(cont. off)* "It's my party and I'll….

(There is a pause. She re-enters another part of the stage.)

...too if it happened to you."

*(We hear the sound and see the light effects of a U.F.O. landing. **R.R.** is revealed.)*

R.R. Hello, Didi.

DIDI. R.R., where in the hell have you been?

R.R. Out and about.

DIDI. I knew you would come back to me. One more day, I would have filed for divorce.

R.R. You can go right ahead with the divorce. I just came back to get some extra fiddle strings.

DIDI. R.R., you've always had a lot of nerve, you know that? Mama always said your gene pool hit a dead end somewhere in Louisiana. Well, let me tell you something. God...

*(**R.R.** snaps his fingers and **DIDI** goes silent, although her lips are still moving. **R.R.** snaps again and **DIDI** speaks.)*

...in here like Rory Calhoun and pull this cowboy crap...

*(**R.R.** snaps again and **DIDI** is silent. He snaps again and **DIDI** speaks.)*

...and I've got another thing to say to you...

*(**R.R.** snaps; **DIDI** cusses violently but silently. They exit. Lights fade to black.)*

End of Act One

ACT II

Scene One

(PEARL walks out of her house, opens an imaginary car door, seats herself and turns the ignition on the car, with no results.)

PEARL. What the...Well, I'll be. Henry's been out here listening to that right-wing idiot and run down the battery again.

(VERA enters on the other side of the stage.)

VERA. *(upset)* Well, Joshua, Judges and Ruth. I threatened Virgil with things out of the Bible if he got near that car and here I am on foot on the most important day of the year. Well, I'm not walking in this heat, this hair will never hold up. Oh, look at Pearl Burras over there making shade.

PEARL. My God. Well, there she is. Vera Carp. Standing out in this heat like a roadrunner looking for a lizard.

VERA. I'd rather vote for Hillary Clinton than ask her for a ride. Hello, Pearl. *(waves)*

PEARL. Hi, Vera. *(waves)*

BOTH. *(simultaneously)* Could I bother you for a ride?

VERA. I'll be right over.

PEARL. What?

VERA. You wouldn't mind giving me a lift to my coronation, would you?

PEARL. I was going to ask you. My car won't start.

VERA. Virgil took off in the Riviera. I hope he's enjoying his last few minutes of freedom. I know what. We can take Lupe's old wagon if you can handle a stick-shift.

PEARL. Oh, I grew up on one.

(VERA gets in the back seat, passenger side, and PEARL gets in the driver's seat of Lupe's car.)

VERA. Hurry up Pearl. What're you waiting for?

PEARL. Where are the keys?

VERA. What?

PEARL. Where are the keys?

VERA. Isn't that just like Lupe not to leave the keys in the car?

PEARL. Get in, Vera. I'll hot wire it.

VERA. What?

(PEARL gets out and opens the hood. VERA gets out, comes around and sits in the driver's seat.)

PEARL. Let me look at this ignition.

VERA. Where did you learn to hot wire cars, Pearl?

PEARL. Henry and I broke down at a prison rodeo one time. You meet the nicest people there.

(PEARL crosses to VERA.)

Here, Vera, you hold these two wires together when I tell you to. *(PEARL returns to the hood.)* All right, Vera, give it a try. *(The ignition almost starts.)* Give her some gas.

(The car starts, and VERA guns the engine. VERA gets out of the driver's seat and PEARL takes her place. VERA then walks around the car and gets in the back seat.)

Why are you sitting in the back seat?

VERA. I'm not getting this hairdo destroyed by an air bag. Hurry up, Pearl. What are you waiting for?

(PEARL takes out her hearing aid and puts it in her purse.)

PEARL. I'm going to take out my hearing aid so I can stand to be in the same small space with you.

VERA. Don't you think you should adjust the rear view mirror?

PEARL. What?

VERA. *(loudly)* Don't you think you should adjust the rear view mirror?

PEARL. No. That thing just throws me off balance. Now, it's been a while since I've driven a standard, but it should be as easy as driving off a cliff.

*(**PEARL** drives the car, shifting gears.)*

VERA. Oh God, that's not how I would have put it. Our Father, Who art in heaven...

PEARL. What?

VERA. Hallowed be Thy name...

PEARL. What about Halloween?

VERA. Thy kingdom come, Thy will be done, on earth as it is in...*(screams.)* Stop sign!

*(**PEARL** slams on the brakes. **VERA** resumes the prayer as **PEARL** drives on.)*

Give us this day our daily... *(screams)...*bread truck!

*(**PEARL** slams on the brakes again.)*

PEARL. Why, that fool nearly hit me!

*(She takes off again. **VERA** sings.)*

VERA. "Still all my songs shall be
Nearer my God to Thee..."

(The sound of another car passing with horn honking is heard.)

Oh, my God, it's Virgil! Look out, Pearl!

PEARL. Hang on, Vera.

(Their car screeches and slams into a ditch with a thud, escaping steam is heard.)

PEARL. That son of yours nearly killed us. I'll never find my partial plate.

VERA. Oh, you're all right. What do you need teeth for?

*(**VERA** gets out and surveys the damage to the car.)*

VERA. *(cont.)* Oh, Lupe is gonna come apart like a cheap *piñata* when she sees what you've done to her car. *(getting back in the car)* Well, I hope you're satisfied. Thanks to you, I'm going to miss my coronation.

PEARL. What about carnations?

VERA. Oh, put in your hearing aid. You sound like something out of Isaiah.

PEARL. I'm going to put my hearing aid in so I can hear the sound of your bones crushing when I get a hold of you.

VERA. Oh, please. You can't even make jello without help.

PEARL. You're right off the Discovery Channel, you know that, Vera? A real night feeder.

VERA. You take that back.

PEARL. All right, I take that back. You're a bottom feeder.

VERA. Well, I'd say something ugly, but God has punished you enough already.

PEARL. By God, Vera, I'm going to show you what happened to the Comanche.

VERA. *(She looks at her watch.)* Oh my God, it's time for the coronation. Turn on the radio, quick.

(**PEARL** *turns on Radio OKKK. We hear* **THURSTON***'s voice on the radio.)*

VOICE OF THURSTON. *(on the radio)* Well folks, we have this just in to the news room. Tuna's new Reunion Queen has just been crowned. And folks, you're not going to believe it. In an upset write-in victory, the new Reunion Queen is Joe Bob Lipsey.

VERA. What!

PEARL. Oh, didn't you know. Didi and I are Joe Bob's campaign managers.

VERA. That's' not the kind of queen we had in mind.

(**VERA** *exits and changes into* **HELEN BEDD***.)*

PEARL. Oh, I don't believe I can stand it.

(A knock is heard in the radio station.)

VOICE OF THURSTON. *(on the radio)* All right, I'm coming, I'm coming. Where's the damn fire?

VOICE OF ARLES. *(on the radio)* Get out of my way, Thurston. Folks, this is Arles Struvie, and I'm locking myself in this radio station until Bertha Bumiller takes me back.

VOICE OF THURSTON. *(on radio)* Folks, he's got a can of hair spray and a cigarette lighter.

VOICE OF ARLES. *(on radio)* Now get out, Thurston. I'm going to play this next song till hell freezes over, or Bertha forgives me, whichever comes first. This one's for you, Baby.

(**ARLES** *starts to play a sad country song, something like "Only the Lonely" by Roy Orbison.* A tire blows. As the song swells,* **PEARL** *exits and changes into* **INITA GOODWIN**.)

Scene Two

(Lights change to reveal the Reunion food booth and a "men" and a "women" rest room sign appear. **HELEN** *enters into food booth carrying her square dance boots. She exits the booth onto the stage and turns the radio music off. We hear* **LEONARD** *over the P.A. system.)*

VOICE OF LEONARD. *(Over the P.A.)* Attention, please, this is Leonard Childers, your local mayor and Master of Ceremonies. Now, it has been ten years since our last high school reunion, and I wanna welcome each of you back home again. We got square dancin', horseshoe pitchin', fiddle playin', cake walks, fishing derbies, fireworks and donkey baseball. Stop by the Smut Snatchers' booth, and catch up on the latest in banned books and videos. And due to the heat, the six-hole golf tournament has been lowered to three. So enjoy the Reunion, stir that lemonade and slice another watermelon.

HELEN. Boy, I hope we didn't forget anything. I tell you, this being our first day on the job and all is working my last nerve.

*(***INITA GOODWIN*** enters into the food booth wearing a Tuna High School letter jacket over a square dance outfit and carrying her square dance boots.)*

INITA. Helen, relax. This new catering business is going to have us minting our own money. And we're gonna win that square dance contest, too.

*(***INITA*** exits the food booth onto stage.)*

HELEN. Oh, look at him. He's cute.

INITA. Not really. Wave at him.

HELEN. *(waves at him)* Ooooh! I've seen more teeth on the front row of a Willie Nelson concert.

INITA. I'm gonna turn the radio on. *(She does. Roy Orbison is singing.*)*

HELEN. He's still in there.

*See MUSIC USE NOTE on page 3

INITA. *(She turns the radio off.)* I hate it that Bertha and Arles broke off their engagement.

HELEN. Oh, look, over there at the yearbook table.

INITA. Oh, it's Fernie and Bernie.

HELEN. They've changed their names to Star and Amber.

INITA. Amber Wind-chime and Star...Star Weather-vane or something.

HELEN. Bird-feather.

INITA. Bird-feather – like she's part Kickapoo.

HELEN. Now, Inita, we need to keep an eye on the food in this heat. We don't want the Board of Health on our case. You know how they are.

INITA. The food is fine. It's been in the back of that truck covered with a tarp for three hours.

HELEN. What about Mrs. Burras' potato salad? You know that's her prize winning recipe.

INITA. It's been right here next to the ice chest for two hours. What could happen to it?

HELEN. I'm so excited about this reunion. All these people coming back to town who never thought we'd amount to a hill of beans, and here we are with our own business.

INITA. And the trailer houses are paid for.

HELEN. And we've only been divorced once each, if you don't count that weekend in Juarez.

INITA. This is great, isn't it, everybody coming back to town, remembering old flames.

HELEN. Like Danny Palvadore?

INITA. I don't know what you're talking about.

HELEN. Girl, you're wearing Danny's old letter jacket in this heat. That jacket's too little for you. You look like you're in traction.

INITA. I don't care.

HELEN. Where in the devil is Garland. When I hired him he promised to be on time and stay off the tequila?

(cell phone rings)

HELEN. Get that will you. I gotta change.

INITA. If I can find that cheap cell phone.

HELEN. You know, that cell phone technology is not at all together. Some old lady in Argentina can fart and my phone rings. I'll be right back.

(HELEN exits and changes to DIDI. INITA finds the cell phone and answers it.)

INITA. Helen and Inita's Hot-to-Trot Catering, Inita speaking, what can I do you for? Oh, hello Ruby....He's here? Danny Palvadore? Is he still cute? Does he have all his hair? Does he still drive that blue Impala? Oh, I'd run a bus load of nuns off the road to get to him again. OK, call you later.

(She hangs up the phone. DIDI enters with great animation.)

Hello, Didi. I'm sorry you didn't win, honey. I voted for you.

(DIDI responds silently and exits and changes to PETEY. INITA calls on the phone.)

Hey, Clayton. Inita. You need to get your ambulance to the reunion right away. We've got our first heat stroke victim. Didi Snavely. No, she's not all right. She's not taking that reunion queen loss well at all. Of course she's packing. She carries a gun to church.

(PETEY enters carrying a large imaginary box.)

PETEY. Hey, Inita.

INITA. Hi, Petey. Petey, you're not really going to get in that hut with all those scorpions, are you?

PETEY. I've got forty-nine of them in this box right here, just need one more.

INITA. You might want to think that over. I got one of those little scorpions in my shoe once, and it stung me half a dozen times before I could get my foot out.

PETEY. Well, what did you expect? That scorpion was just defending its space. It had no choice. How would you react if a huge foot twenty times your size came crashing into your living space?

INITA. Petey, does mental illness run in your family?

PETEY. Thanks a lot for the moral support, Inita. *(He opens the top of the box and speaks to the scorpions as he exits.)* Don't listen to her, fellas. She can't help it. She was brought up that way. Ow!

(PETEY exits and changes to GARLAND.)

INITA. I gotta practice. *(She practices her square dance.)*
> Allemande left with the old left hand,
> Meet your honey in a right left grand.
> Right left grand, Right left grand.

Oh shoot. I forgot my foot powder. I'll never get these boots on. There's Garland. Hey, Garland. You're late. Garland. Get in here, baby. I need your help.

(We hear GARLAND offstage.)

GARLAND. *(offstage)* Hey, Inita.

INITA. Listen, Garland, you still owe me a favor for leaving me passed out in the back of the truck last Christmas.

(GARLAND enters into the food booth.)

GARLAND. I couldn't get a grip on you. You were all covered in frost. *(He laughs.)*

INITA. You watch the food booth for a second. I gotta go to my truck and get some foot powder.

GARLAND. *(laughs)* Good. How are you going to pay me back?

INITA. Have some potato salad on me, and we'll take the rest out in trade.

GARLAND. *(laughs)* You crack me up, Inita, you know that?

(INITA exits and changes to LEONARD. GARLAND calls off.)

Hey Leonard, get over here and have some of Pearl's potato salad.

Hey Grady! Better get out of this heat with your condition.

(GARLAND has turned on "Only the Lonely" on the radio. He likes it. A bottle rocket goes by his head and he turns off the radio.)

GARLAND. *(cont.)* Hey! Hey! Virgil Carp. You fire off another bottle rocket and I'll stick you on the grill with the rest of the weenies. *(Another rocket goes by.* GARLAND *ducks.)* Virgil, I'm serious. I'm not afraid of your old man. I don't owe the bank any money.

(GARLAND turns the radio back on. LEONARD *enters immediately.)*

LEONARD. Turn that damn thing off, Garland, hell! Have a little mercy. Today's not the day to own a radio station.

GARLAND. *(turns off the radio)* You seem a little upset, Leonard.

LEONARD. Oh, does it show? You lose four hours of paid advertising on the biggest damn day of the year. Now, give me something to drink. And I don't mean R.C. Cola.

GARLAND. All I see is Tequila.

LEONARD. That'll work. *(GARLAND pours a shot for* LEONARD.*)* What I really need is some of that illegal substance that they sell on the streets of Houston. I'd inject it right here into my temple and go visit Hank Williams, Senior. *(They do the shots.)* Is that Pearl's potato salad? Give me some.

GARLAND. *(dishing out salad)* Everybody else seems to be having a real good time, Leonard.

LEONARD. To hell with everyone else. *(A bottle rocket swooshes by.)* Now cut that out. Somebody needs to do something about these damn kids!

GARLAND. *(He pours another round.)* Don't hold that in, Leonard, it'll kill you.

LEONARD. Who else would be the mayor of this half-assed hole in the road we call a town?

GARLAND. How do you really feel? *(*GARLAND *laughs.)*

LEONARD. Laugh all you want, but there ain't gonna be no homecoming float.

GARLAND. Why not?

LEONARD. Dixie Deberry won't let Joe Bob on the float. The county insurance plan won't cover a queen that big on a bale that high.

(They do another shot.)

I'll never get re-elected mayor, and Stanley Bumiller should be shipped off to Devil's Island for what he's done to me.

GARLAND. What's ol' Stanley done now?

LEONARD. Oh, that piece of art he gave the town. And I, like a damn idiot, agreed to unveil it.

(A bottle-rocket whizzes by, and **LEONARD** *ducks it.)*

Who did that?

GARLAND. That little pea-brain, Virgil Carp.

LEONARD. You know, Garland, there was a time you could legally kill kids.

GARLAND. Go on about Stanley's art.

LEONARD. You call that art? I call it character assassination. You know what was underneath of that sheet?

GARLAND. *(laughs)* What?

LEONARD. Half a dozen coyotes wearing women's dresses and hats, sitting on a church pew. The one in the yellow moomoo looked a lot like my wife.

GARLAND. *(goes wild laughing)* Damn, that's funny.

LEONARD. I laughed, too, when I first saw those coyotes. One of them was the spittin' image of Vera Carp. She had a chicken wing sticking out of her purse. Then I saw those Smut Snatchers milling around with their teeth all bared. They'll never give me another endorsement for mayor. And my wife is on the verge of killing half the members of Free White Texas. *(He belches.)* You know, Garland, that potato salad tasted a little ripe. Damn, I gotta go in there and ride the old porcelain pony.

*(***LEONARD*** exits into the men's rest room and changes to* **INITA.***)*

GARLAND. You've still got my vote, Leonard.

(He laughs, does another shot, then the cell phone rings and he answers it.)

Helen and Inita's Hot to Trot Catering, Garland speaking. No, we don't have no egg rolls. No, we don't have no shish-ka-bob. We've got potato salad. Well, it's a little tangy, but that's the way I like it. Pizza? Woman, if you want Mexican food you've got the wrong number. *(He hangs up, does one more shot.)* Um…. Um…. Uh oh.

(GARLAND exits booth and changes to Vera.)

Inita, Baby, you need to take over for me. I need some help.

(INITA enters into food booth.)

INITA. What's wrong with you Garland? Where are you going? You just got here.

GARLAND. *(offstage)* I need to go lie down for a minute. I feel funny.

INITA. You always feel funny.

GARLAND. Not ha-ha funny. Like, like-I'm-gonna-die funny. You might want to take a whiff of that potato salad.

INITA. *(She tastes it.)* It tastes all right to me. It's a little tangy, but that's the way I like it. *(She looks off.)* Oh no, Garland, don't lie in the street like that. *(She grabs the imaginary tequila bottle.)* Hold on, baby. What you need is a shot of tequila.

(She exits the booth and changes to SPIKES. VERA enters wearing a real bullhorn on a strap around her neck. She looks at her watch.)

VERA. Where is he? Where in the gumption is Reverend Spikes? He's always late when he first gets out of jail. Prison leaves him with no concept of time.

(VERA walks by the food booth. She sniffs the air.)

Lord, that potato salad has gone bad. I'd better toss that out. Somebody might eat it.

(She starts to dump the potato salad, catches herself and stops.)

VERA. *(cont.)* Well, maybe not. People in this town voted for that yard sale Liberace for Reunion Queen. They can just fend for themselves and God can sort out the survivors.

(She speaks into the bullhorn.)

Attention all sinners. No matter what kind of scum you are you can become a loving Christian just like me. Attention all sinners.

*(**REVEREND STURGIS SPIKES** enters.)*

Well there you are. I always worry when you're late. I'm afraid the cops have picked you up again.

SPIKES. Now Vera, let's not get started off on the wrong hoof here.

VERA. Don't cross me on a day like today. I lost my rightful place on that hay bale, and my best friend's been jilted by a gin-soaked Methodist. So I don't need some Elmer Gantry attitude from you.

SPIKES. We're not drawing much of a crowd.

VERA. Maybe we should sing some of those new cleaned up bible school songs.

SPIKES. Good idea, Vera. What have we got?

VERA. Well, I've got the new lyrics here to "Jesus Loves Me."

SPIKES. Did the committee reach a decision on the new words?

VERA. Yes, we sought the Lord's guidance in rewriting His hymns without messing up the rhyme scheme. I'll sing while you pass out flyers.

SPIKES. Just a minute, Vera, I want to get a bite of that potato salad first.

VERA. Oh no. Don't do that unless you know you're right with God.

SPIKES. Sing, Vera.

*(**VERA** sings into the bullhorn.)*

VERA. "Jesus loves me, I can see
     Cause his picture's just like me.
     Pale white skin, blond hair, blue eyes,
     It should come as no surprise."

SPIKES. We're never gonna draw a crowd with singing like that.

VERA. Maybe you'd like to lead us all in a verse of Folsom Prison Blues.

SPIKES. Vera, I'll have you know I'm never closer to God than when I'm in prison. A little hard time might do you some good, Vera.

VERA. It's a hard time just looking at your sad face.

(A siren is heard getting louder.)

SPIKES. I didn't do it. I was nowhere near wherever it was.

*(***SPIKES*** *runs off and changes to* **JOE BOB.***)*

VERA. It's not the police, it's an ambulance. If you weren't so guilty you wouldn't be so nervous, you born again has been. *(A bottle rocket whizzes past her. She yells through the bullhorn to* **VIRGIL.***)* Virgil Carp. Virgil Carp. I see you hiding behind that dumpster. Young man, you are to leave the keys in the Riviera and walk home and wait for my decision about your future. Don't you dare sulk at me. You pick up that big ugly lip. Lord, you were an ugly baby and you're still ugly. I mean it, Virgil. You're going to do more walking than John the Baptist in the wilderness. March. Now. I tell you, if it wasn't for my faith, a day like today would have me knitting doilies on death row.

*(***JOE BOB LIPSEY*** *enters singing, dressed as the Reunion Queen.)*

JOE BOB. "I get no kick from champagne…"

VERA. Hello, Joe Bob.

JOE BOB. Oh Vera Carp, or Miss Better Luck Next Time, I shower my condolences upon you. *(goes to the foodbooth and calls off)* Does anyone work here? We need food!

VERA. Joe Bob, don't you think you're getting a little too big for your hay bale?

JOE BOB. You stay away from me, you chicken fried Eva Braun. *(He calls off.)* We must have food! We're hypoglycaemic!

VERA. Joe Bob, I don't think nourishment is the big issue here. You're going to have to walk that parade route. If I were you I'd run home and put on some sensible shoes.

JOE BOB. You are giving me fashion advice?

VERA. Well, when you're uninsurable, you better learn how to accessorize. You won't make it past the stop light in those plywood flip-flops.

JOE BOB. That coming from a woman whose feet could feed a family of cannibals for a week.

VERA. Poor thing. Always got food on the mind.

JOE BOB. Vera, you just can't admit that democracy has kicked your ass.

VERA. You better watch your potty mouth. You sound like you've been reading Doonesbury.

JOE BOB. I love Doonesbury.

VERA. Well, read it quick. It's going on our constitutional hit list. Right behind Sponge Bob.

JOE BOB. Democracy has spoken!

VERA. That's so quaint. Everybody knows democracy keeps its mouth shut till the lawyers are out for the recount. Mine's due in forty-five minutes. Who have you retained?

JOE BOB. Well, Vera, I have to go pose for the photographers and I'm sure you're needed back at the coven.

VERA. Joe Bob, wait. My Christian upbringing won't allow me to see you go hungry. Here, you have some potato salad. I'll pay for it.

*(**VERA** goes into the food booth and serves **JOE BOB** a bowl of potato salad.)*

JOE BOB. *(exiting)* Well, thank you, Vera. That's very nice of you. Mm, tangy, just like I like it.

VERA. Just watching you eat it gives me the joy, joy, joy down in my heart.

(JOE BOB exits. A bottle rocket whizzes by and goes into the food booth, ricocheting off the walls.)

Virgil, you'd better be ready for the rapture, 'cause I'm coming after you in a very Christian way!

(VERA exits food booth onto stage and off, changes to HELEN. JOE BOB re-enters, exits into the women's room. HELEN screams off from the women's room. JOE BOB re-enters from the women's room and exits into the men's room.)

LEONARD. *(offstage from men's room)* Hey, hey! Get out of here!

(JOE BOB exits men's room and goes off, changes to R.R. The cell phone rings. HELEN enters from women's room.)

HELEN. Boy, he puts on open-backed shoes and thinks he can just walk in anywhere. *(answers the phone)* Helen and Inita's Hot-to-Trot Catering. How may I help you?… No, this isn't the police. Well, don't start crying. Who is this? Consuela Garcia? You're calling from Vera Carp's house? Oh, you must be the new Lupe. Somebody stole your car? Oh no. And they wrecked it? Oh no. Do you know who did it? Vera Carp? She left her lipstick in the back seat. Well, call the cops. No, do it, girl. Nuevo Uno Uno. No, Lupe. You got the same rights as anybody else in this country to hire a sleezewod lawyer and go to court and make your fellow American's life a living hell. Nuevo Uno Uno? Go get 'em, girl.

(R.R. enters.)

R.R. what are you doing here?

R.R. I just came by for a barbecue sandwich.

HELEN. Chopped or sliced?

R.R. Half and half.

HELEN. So where have you been hiding for the last few years?

R.R. I'd tell you but you'd call me nuts.

HELEN. Oh, I'd never do that.

R.R. Well, I've been all over the galaxy in a space ship.

HELEN. Uh huh. Did you go to the moon?

R.R. Oh, now our moon isn't much. Now Jupiter has sixteen moons.

HELEN. Uh huh. Does Didi know you're back?

R.R. Yeah.

HELEN. What did she have to say?

R.R. Not much. You're not going to tell everybody I'm nuts are you?

HELEN. Oh, I'd never do that, R.R.

R.R. Thanks, Helen.

(R.R. exits and changes to **STAR.***)*

HELEN. Bye R.R. *(HELEN calls Veda Jo on the cell phone.)* Veda Jo, you'll never guess who just walked up to the food booth...R.R. Snavely...No, he's not all right. He's nuts...Well, you need to hurry up. You're gonna miss all the fun. Oh it's a wonderful reunion...Well, it's a little hot...about 110, but it's a dry heat. And guess who got Reunion Queen. Joe Bob Lipsey. Can you believe it? I thought I was the only one to write him in. Hello...Hello...I hate it when these cell phones cut you off like that.

(HELEN sees somebody off stage. She squeals.)

(calling off) Bonnie Jean! It's me, Helen Bedd. Can you believe it? I'll be right there. Somebody watch the place, will you?

(HELEN exits and changes to **AMBER.** **STAR BIRD-FEATHER** *enters.)*

STAR. God, I hope this food booth has some trail mix. I've never seen so much cooked flesh in all my life. *(A bottle-rocket whizzes by.)* Wow! That is so micro-cosmically militaristic. I'm starving. There must be something I can eat. Oh no, baby-back ribs. Poor piggies. Chili. Poor Cows. Hot dogs. Poor...who knows. I need some music.

(She moves to **HELEN***'s radio and turns it on. Roy is still singing "Only the Lonely."* She turns it off.)*

STAR. *(cont.)* I am in the Twilight Zone.

(AMBER WIND-CHIME *enters in a state.)*

AMBER. Oh, Star.

STAR. Amber, your aura is very weak.

AMBER. Oh, Star, someone left the cake out in the rain.

STAR. What happened to bring you so far down?

AMBER. *(She begins a ritual of putting Patchouli on her wrists and eye drops in her eyes.)* Well, first of all, Connie Carp comes up and proves that she's still the same sweat-hog after all these years.

STAR. What did she say?

AMBER. Star, this really hurts. She asked me if I knew that the sixties were over.

STAR. Heavy. What did you say?

AMBER. I asked her if she had ever heard of unsaturated fat.

STAR. Did that bring you down to say that?

AMBER. Are you kidding? I dropped an entire chakra level. And then Paula Polk comes up and asked me if I was still a vegetarian, and I said yes, and she asked me if I wanted to taste her guacamole, and I ate a whole spoonful, and do you know what that she-hog had done?

STAR. What?

AMBER. She'd put bacon in it.

STAR. That is so heavy.

AMBER. They didn't even eat bacon in the Bible.

STAR. I didn't know that. You are so well read.

AMBER. And Star.

*See MUSIC USE NOTE on page 3

STAR. Yeah?

AMBER. Do you know what was worse?

STAR. What?

AMBER. It tasted so good.

STAR. Amber, go sit in the car and hum.

AMBER. Oh no. Star, you're going to have to take my hand and lead the way.

STAR. Why?

AMBER. I can't believe I put patchouli in my eyes again.

STAR. Hum, Amber, hum.

> (**AMBER** *exits, humming, and changes to* **STANLEY**.)

There's one other person I want to see, and then we'll drive to New Mexico to Rainbow and Moach-cha's sweat lodge and purge that clove-footed animal from your system.

> (*The cell phone rings.* **STAR** *answers the phone.*)

Hello…I don't know. Like there's nobody here… Look, I don't know. What are you, a triple Scorpio?

> (*She hangs up. A bunch of firecrackers is heard exploding offstage.* **STANLEY** *enters, shaking his head. The sun begins to set.*)

Who's that mean kid?

STANLEY. Oh man, it's that little idgit, Virgil Carp. He threw a whole roll of firecrackers under that hut where Petey is locked in with all those scorpions.

STAR. Uncool. Did they sting him?

STANLEY. Yeah, he's jumping around like Richard Simmons. Petey Fisk is too good for this town. He ought to move to New Mexico with me.

STAR. You know, I'm going to New Mexico later today. I'm taking my friend Amber to a sweat lodge and have her purged.

STANLEY. Whoa. I just recognized you. You're Bernice Snodgrass.

STAR. Yes, well, I used to be.

STANLEY. *(introducing himself)* Hi. I'm Stanley Bumiller.

STAR. Yes, I know.

STANLEY. So, I guess you got married?

STAR. Yes, but I changed my name before that to Star Bird-feather because I had to, like, shed my past, if you know what I mean.

STANLEY. Boy, do I. Is your husband here?

STAR. No, he died on a religious retreat to the Himalayas.

STANLEY. Mountain climbing?

STAR. Bad yak butter.

STANLEY. Beats the hell out of dying of boredom in a place like this.

STAR. Well, I don't know. Electing a man Reunion Queen is a step in the cosmic direction.

STANLEY. Joe Bob will be lucky to get out of town alive if the Smut Snatchers catch him.

STAR. I forgot how heavy this town is.

STANLEY. That's something I figured out a long time ago. *(a pause)* Do you know you're the only person in this town who wrote me while I was in reform school, except for my momma? I appreciate it, I really do.

STAR. I knew you were going to be a great artist some day. I could see you had talent back when you were spray-painting stop signs. I never liked stop signs. They are so abrupt. I always thought they should at least say "Please." But I liked them after you painted them.

STANLEY. That's why Judge Buckner threw me in reform school, for spray painting stop signs.

STAR. Well, being sent to reform school is no worse than being found dead in a woman's swim suit like he was. That's where they should send that Virgil Carp for what he did to Petey.

STANLEY. Yeah, well, rich kids don't go to reform school.

STAR. Where do they go?

STANLEY. SMU. Boy, would you look at that. Even Tuna can't screw up a West Texas sunset.

STAR. That's my favorite thing about the West.

STANLEY. So when are you heading back to New Mexico.

STAR. As soon as I can get directions. I know its somewhere to the left.

STANLEY. Well, now that my momma's wedding's off, I'm heading that way in a little while. You want to follow me? I gotta say goodbye to my Aunt Pearl first.

STAR. Cool. I'll go tell Amber.

STANLEY. Do I know Amber?

STAR. Fern Posey. But don't call her that. She's real fragile today.

STANLEY. I remember her. She and I got thrown out of vacation Bible school for playing strip poker in the fellowship hall.

STAR. You were so cool.

STANLEY. We'll see you back here in about an hour?

STAR. Cool.

STANLEY. Cool.

(*They exit.* STANLEY *changes to* HELEN. STAR *changes to* INITA. THURSTON'*s voice is heard over the PA system.*)

VOICE OF THURSTON. (*over PA*) Attention all residents and visitors. Please listen carefully. If you or anyone you know has come in contact with potato salad from Helen and Inita's Hot-to-Trot catering, you are advised to adhere to the following instructions. Do not eat or drink anything, avoid confined, unventilated spaces including automobiles, and stay within ten feet of the nearest public facilities. Cots are being set up in the Tuna High gymnasium where victims can receive medical attention and consult with personal injury attorneys.

(HELEN *enters followed by* INITA.)

INITA. Helen, give me that potato salad.

HELEN. Stay away from that, girl. It's gone bad.

INITA. I know that. I'm gonna eat half a pound of it and die right here, where Danny Palvadore can find my body. Helen, you can't believe what that man did to me.

HELEN. Oh, no. Girl, did he ignore you?

INITA. Worse.

HELEN. Did he laugh at your outfit?

INITA. Worse.

HELEN. Did he make fun of your hairdo?

INITA. Worse.

HELEN. Did he mention that you'd gained weight?

INITA. ...Worse.

HELEN. What did he do?

INITA. *(starting to sob)* He apologized to me.

HELEN. Apologized for what?

INITA. Everything. He apologized for the fifty yard line.

HELEN. No.

INITA. He apologized for the cotton trailers.

HELEN. Uh uh. Girl, he didn't apologize for leaving you in that tree.

INITA. Yes.

HELEN. Men can be so cruel.

INITA. I'm never gonna look at another man as long as I live.

HELEN. Girl.

INITA. And I'm never gonna cook again either.

HELEN. Girl.

INITA. I mean it. I'll probably get hauled in for that potato salad.

HELEN. That wasn't premeditated. The worst you can get is manslaughter.

INITA. I mean it. No more men and no more cookin'. We gotta move fast before the cops get here. You gas up the truck and I'll pull the blocks out from under the trailer house. Danny Palvadore can kiss my ass.

HELEN. Wait a minute. This is a big moment for us. I think we owe Tuna one last look before we go.

INITA. You're right, Helen. It's the end of an era.

(They pause and look around for 4 seconds.)

HELEN. OK, that's enough. Let's go. Inita, grab that potato salad. We don't want to leave any evidence if the cops arrive.

INITA. *(grabbing the salad)* Time to hit the road, Jack.

*(They exit laughing and singing "Hit the Road, Jack." ***HELEN** *changes to* **DIDI.** **INITA** *changes to* **R.R.** *The food booth goes away and we are outside. The stars come out and the radio light comes on. We hear a little of "Hit the Road, Jack," then* **THURSTON** *on the radio.)*

VOICE OF THURSTON. *(on radio)* This is Thurston Wheelis back at last on Radio Station OKKK and I'm not sure where Arles is. And after listening to that song all day long, I could care less. Well, it's been quite a reunion, and except for the heat strokes, snake bites, scorpion stings, food poisonings and Vera Carp's arrest for grand theft auto, a good time was had by all. And don't forget we've still got our live coverage of the fireworks display at Jaguar Stadium. We'll see you there.

(The Radio Light goes out.)

\

*See MUSIC USE NOTE on page 3

Scene Three

(**R.R.** *enters, looking at the stars.* **DIDI** *enters and sees him.*)

R.R. I know you're mad, Didi, and you want to get that divorce. Well, you can go right ahead and get it because I'm already remarried. Once I got picked up by the space ship, I was only subject to intergalactic law.

(**R.R.** *snaps and* **DIDI** *speaks.*)

DIDI. I'm gonna go in the house and I'm gonna get my sawed off uzi, and I'm gonna blow your cheatin' ass away. God…

(**R.R.** *snaps her.* **DIDI** *exits and changes to* **PETEY.** **R.R.** *stretches out his arms, points his fingers toward her and makes a waving gesture.*)

R.R. That'll keep her put

(*He looks at his watch, then looks off sees* **PETEY** *off stage.*)

And there's Petey right on time.

(**PETEY** *enters.*)

PETEY. Hey, R.R., I appreciate your doing this. Come on, you guys, catch up. It's just R.R.; you remember him. He's taking you with him.

R.R. Is this all of them?

PETEY. Most. Some didn't want to leave earth. What's wrong with you, Fresno? What are you growling at? Is that Didi over there? Why is she frozen like that?

R.R. I've got her on ice, but we got to hurry.

PETEY. Come on, everybody. Now, Nedra, relax. R.R. says there's lots of snakes where he's going.

R.R. Is she a python?

PETEY. No, she's just a big rattle snake born without fangs. It wreaks havoc on her self esteem. Come on, Paula, iguanas too.

R.R. That's a cute little alligator behind Paula.

PETEY. That's Percy. He's had a rough time here on the desert. You have to make sure they bunk together; lizards are clannish.

R.R. Is something wrong with that rabbit?

PETEY. Oh, Judy? She won't breed.

R.R. Is she sick?

PETEY. No, just real picky.

R.R. I don't think Fresno wants to go.

PETEY. Let me talk to him. Come here, Fresno. There's nothing to be afraid of. Where you're going nobody will be shooting at you from a helicopter. You don't want to stay here. This place has just gone from mean to meaner, full of bad losers and worse winners. They've got a huntin' season for everything short of mosquitoes. They chop down trees like they were communists, and exterminators are serving in Congress. You're going to where nobody can hurt you. You can be a coyote without the consequences. After global warming, R.R. can bring you back to repopulate the earth. Nobody's likely to survive that but cockroaches and coyotes. Well, Madonna will probably make it.

R.R. We better move quick. I've got Didi on a timer.

(**R.R.** *calls his spaceship with accompanying high tech sound. It lands.*)

PETEY. Allright, all of you, let's go. Hurry up.

R.R. We'll meet here from time to time, and I'll take on all the ones you can't place.

PETEY. I'd like to go with you, R.R.

R.R. They need you down here, Petey.

PETEY. Oh yeah. Bye, R.R.

R.R. See you, Petey.

(**PETEY** *exits and changes to* **STANLEY**. **R.R.** *snaps his fingers and exits into the UFO and changes to* **PEARL**. *We hear* **DIDI** *off.*)

DIDI. *(off)* …dammit!

(The space ship takes off. There is a silence, followed by a lighting effect of a fireworks display, complete with sound effects – three pops and a moderately loud fizzle and boom.

Scene Four

(Lights come up first inside and on the radio, then on Pearl's Boudoir. PEARL enters and makes her bed from four chairs.)

VOICE OF THURSTON. *(on radio)* This is Thurston Wheelis with your live, on-the-scene coverage of Tuna's Fourth-of-July fireworks display, and as you just heard, the whole she-bang took less than thirty seconds. That's because Virgil Carp got into the fireworks and all we had left were three sky rockets and a wet cherry bomb. So that, as they say, is that. And here's a final update on that Free White Texas hostage crisis. As you know, Reba Childers had demanded a $400 fee for the release of the hostages to cover rug damage, or she said she would kill them. And we have confirmed that the organization was able to raise $375 and promised Reba to deliver the other twenty five as soon as the bank opens tomorrow morning. Services are pending at Hubert Funeral Home. This is Thurston Wheelis on Radio Station OKKK signing off.

(PEARL turns off the radio and gets into bed. STANLEY enters.)

STANLEY. Pearl, what are you doing in bed so early?

PEARL. Stanley, I want you to promise me something in my final hours.

STANLEY. Final hours? What are you talking about?

PEARL. It's the funeral home – don't let them cut and bob my hair. I've always liked what little I've had.

STANLEY. Hell, Pearl. You're funny as a crutch. You're not dying.

PEARL. Oh, I've been murdered by humiliation.

STANLEY. Well, Pearl, you have to look on the bright side. At least Vera didn't get it, and she's in jail to boot.

PEARL. It's only a matter of time till they come for me. I'm the one that hot-wired that car. Don't let them put me in a cell with her. That's cruel and unusual punishment. Oh, and another thing, Stanley, whatever you do, don't let them bury me in a house coat.

STANLEY. What?

PEARL. When my cousin, Mabel, died, her family went through her things so fast they had to bury her in a pink house coat. I thought she was going to get up and clean. And music – I want to hear "In the Sweet By and By" and "Blessed Assurance." And don't forget "Amazing Grace." You can't put me in the ground until they sing "Amazing Grace."

STANLEY. That's the only hymn that didn't scare me as a kid, "Amazing Grace." All those other old songs that folks sang at church gave me the shakes. "Amazing Grace" always made me feel like somebody. *(pause)* I don't know what I'm trying to say.

PEARL. Stanley, you're growing up.

STANLEY. I guess.

PEARL. Oh God, Stanley! I see a light!

STANLEY. That's a car passing, Pearl.

(pause)

PEARL. You know, Stanley, when I was a girl some folks were still being hauled around in wagons. And the prairie was littered with buffalo skulls. And now we've got people going to the Moon and Mars. Do you think those pictures they show on TV are really from Mars?

STANLEY. I doubt it. Looks a lot like Arizona to me. I keep expecting to see a Stuckey's.

PEARL. Everything has changed, and yet it's still the same. I won't miss folks much, except for you. I knew you would turn out right if you got away from this town and started over where folks would give you a chance. I'll miss you, Stanley.

STANLEY. Pearl, you're not going to die. But I gotta hit the road in a little while, and I've got to get something off my chest. You're the only one I can trust to tell me what to do.

PEARL. You better hurry, Honey. I could go any minute.

(There is a pause.)

STANLEY. I killed Judge Buckner.

PEARL. You know that's not true. He died of a massive coronary brought on by meanness. I'm so glad they found him dead wearing a woman's swimsuit.

STANLEY. That heart attack was brought on by a hypodermic needle full of air that I shot into one of his veins first thing that morning. I killed him.

PEARL. Oh, no, Honey. He died the night before. Cooter Wooten told me that. She's the county coroner, you know. She said he'd been dead for fifteen hours when the maid found him. She said he was so stiff they had to break his legs to get him in the coffin. It was just awful. I wish I could have been there.

STANLEY. You mean…? He must have been dead before I got to him. No wonder it was so hard to get him in that swimsuit.

PEARL. You did that?

STANLEY. Yeah.

PEARL. I'm so glad. You've always had such a creative spirit, Stanley. You get that from my side of the family. Try not to miss me when I'm gone.

STANLEY. Pearl, I'm surprised at you, going on like this, after what you told me this morning. You've got lots to live for. I admit I had some trouble with it this morning, and then I got to thinking and I realized that you shouldn't give up something so special and fun just because you get old. As long as you can feel love, you should experience it as often as you want to.

PEARL. That's beautiful.

STANLEY. It makes perfect sense to me, as long as you keep the lights off.

PEARL. Oh, your uncle Henry won't even take off his socks if the lights are on. I've been married to him all these years and I've never seen his feet.

STANLEY. Yeah, I guess it will be real hard on Uncle Henry with you gone and all. It will probably take him a while to find someone else.

PEARL. What?

STANLEY. Well, you can't expect Uncle Henry to give up all his pleasure in life just because you decided to lay down and croak. I'm sure there's another woman out there somewhere.

PEARL. Well, she'll be climbing out of bed with a limp if she touches my husband. Help me up, Stanley, give me my cane.

(STANLEY helps her up.)

Now you go out to the den and wake up your Uncle Henry, and then run along. *(She moves to a chest of drawers and looks inside.)* I've got to find it.

STANLEY. Find what, Pearl?

PEARL. That nightgown that I ordered from *Field and Stream* magazine, it's got all these hunting dogs on it. It just drives Henry wild.

STANLEY. Hell, Pearl, you're crazy.

PEARL. Don't say that, Stanley, I'm not.

*(Lights fade. **STANLEY** changes to **ARLES** and **PEARL** changes to **BERTHA** on stage.)*

Scene Five

(We hear a reprise of "Misty" as lights come up on the honeymoon suite at the Starlight Motel in Sand City, Texas. **ARLES** and **BERTHA** enter and stand on either side of the bed.)*

BERTHA. Well, here we are.

ARLES. Yep, here we are. *(There is a pause.)* Right here.

BERTHA. Arles, thank you for the flowers. I'm so glad you could find some on such short notice. I just wouldn't feel like a bride without flowers.

ARLES. It's a good thing that grocery store was open. You have to think fast when you elope.

BERTHA. And the Justice of the Peace was so nice, and his wife knew all the words to "Misty." Who would have imagined that?

ARLES. She sure could play that accordion.

BERTHA. Oh, my, yes. She went to town on that accordion.

ARLES. And I thought their kids lighting those sparklers as we left was a nice touch.

BERTHA. Oh, and Arles, thank you for going by the car wash and getting all that writing off the back window. What was it they wrote back there?

ARLES. They said, "It'll be a hot time in the old gown tonight."

BERTHA. Lord, I hope nobody noticed that.

ARLES. I don't think so. The whole town was out at the stockyards watching the fireworks.

(Pause. They sit on the bed.)

BERTHA. Well, here we are.

ARLES. Yeah. Here we are. *(There is a pause. He pats the bed.)* Nice firm mattress.

BERTHA. Uh-huh. Nice and firm. *(She gently bounces on the bed.)*

(They start speaking at the same time.)

I don't like them too firm.

*See MUSIC USE NOTE on page 3

ARLES. I like 'em real firm. *(replies to Bertha's comment)* You don't?

BERTHA. Oh, this one is fine, just fine.

ARLES. I can call the desk and have them bring another.

BERTHA. No, no.

ARLES. You know what the desk clerk said about satisfaction being guaranteed. I can help him bring in another mattress if that's what you want.

BERTHA. I wouldn't think of it. This one is just fine. Nice and firm.

ARLES. Firm.

(**ARLES** *puts his feet up on the bed, as does* **BERTHA**. *There is a pause.*)

BERTHA. Pretty wallpaper.

ARLES. Uh-huh. *(pause)* Real pretty.

BERTHA. I like yellow.

ARLES. Goes good with your hair.

BERTHA. Thank you. *(She looks up at the ceiling.)* What is that hanging from the ceiling?

ARLES. I expect those bolts used to hold a mirror up there.

BERTHA. A mirror? Why would anybody hang a mirror above a bed?

ARLES. Well, it is a honeymoon suite.

BERTHA. *(Thinks for a moment then gets it.)* Oh, my, I could never watch that. I'd have to wear sunglasses or something. I'd be worried to death it would fall.

ARLES. *(laughs)* Well, that's not the way like I'd like to be found, sandwiched between my bride and a two hundred pound mirror.

(*They both laugh. There is a pause.* **BERTHA** *reaches over to her night stand, takes a pill and washes it down with water.*)

ARLES. That's not a hormone pill, is it?

BERTHA. *(surprised)* No. It's for my acid reflux.

ARLES. Thank God almighty. I want you to promise me something.

BERTHA. What?

ARLES. If the doctor ever puts you on hormones, I want you to promise to tell me and for God sakes promise to take them.

BERTHA. Why?

ARLES. Just promise, I've travelled this route before.

BERTHA. All right, I promise.

ARLES. Trudy used to get mad and refused to take her hormones.

BERTHA. Did that make her mean?

ARLES. Mean? Mean with back hair. It got so bad when she refused to take 'em, hell, I'd take 'em instead.

BERTHA. Arles!

ARLES. Hell, one of us had to have some relief.

BERTHA. Did they affect you?

ARLES. I didn't notice much change. I started going to a lot of Julia Roberts's movies. *(He laughs, she doesn't.)* That's a joke.

BERTHA. I don't get it.

ARLES. Let's just let it pass.

(There is a pause. BERTHA hiccups.)

Are you all right?

BERTHA. This happens whenever I get nervous. *(She hiccups.)*

ARLES. Can I do anything for you?

BERTHA. Distract me. If I put my mind on something else it will stop. *(She hiccups.)*

ARLES. Okay. *(He searches for a subject.)* Nice big TV.

(BERTHA hiccups.)

Two hundred channels. You want me to turn it on?

BERTHA. No, I'm fine. *(She hiccups.)*

ARLES. We can find out about the weather in Arkansas, see what it's going to be like when we get there.

BERTHA. No, I'd rather be surprised. *(She hiccups.)* Thank you, Arles, for agreeing to take me to Eureka Springs. I know you'll like it.

ARLES. I just want you to be happy, Baby.

(**BERTHA** *hiccups.* **ARLES** *puts his hand behind* **BERTHA** *and touches her. She screams.)*

I'm sorry.

BERTHA. Oh, that scared me.

ARLES. Why?

BERTHA. Well, I didn't know who it was.

ARLES. Nobody here but us chickens. *(laughs)* That's another joke.

BERTHA. I don't get that one either.

ARLES. Well, it's not supposed to be comedy night at the Grand Ole Opry. It's supposed to be a wedding bed.

BERTHA. Well, excuse me, but it's been a long time since I've been in a wedding bed.

ARLES. Well, it's not something I'd think you'd forget. It's like riding a bicycle.

BERTHA. I never got the hang of a bicycle.

ARLES. Great.

BERTHA. Arles, don't get mouthy with me.

ARLES. I'm not getting mouthy with you. All I did was touch you.

BERTHA. And I told you I didn't know who it was.

ARLES. Who in the hell did you think it was? *(He looks under the bed and yells under it.)* All right, everybody out!

BERTHA. That's not funny.

ARLES. I couldn't agree more. *(There is a pause.)* Well, we might as well see what's on the tube.

BERTHA. Don't you dare. I'm not spending my honeymoon watching Greta Van What's-her-chops.

ARLES. Well what would you like to do? I've got a Frisbee in the car.

BERTHA. I'm sorry, Arles. I'm nervous because I want it to be beautiful this time. I was so infatuated with Hank, and he treated me like a retread. I spent my whole life waiting on that man, waiting for him to get home from work, waiting for him to show up at the hospital when the twins were born, which he never did, waiting for him to get out of prison.

ARLES. You know, one time I waited three months for Trudy to come home from the grocery store. She left one night to get cigarettes, said she'd be back in ten minutes, and it took me three months to find her.

BERTHA. Where'd you find her?

ARLES. Playing bingo on an Indian reservation in Oklahoma.

BERTHA. Oh, my. What did she say when you found her?

ARLES. She asked me for a cigarette.

BERTHA. Oh.

ARLES. We never did find the car.

BERTHA. Well, we both deserve better. I think this new marriage should offer us something different, don't you agree?

ARLES. One hundred percent. And I've got just what we need right here. *(He pulls out a book.)*

BERTHA. What is it?

ARLES. It's a book about healthy sexual relationships between a husband and wife that I got from my cousin Slim.

BERTHA. The preacher?

ARLES. Yep.

BERTHA. Let me see that. *(She takes the book and starts leafing through it.)* Would you look at the size of that word. It's too big for Wheel of Fortune.

ARLES. Read what it says there.

(BERTHA reads.)

BERTHA. Oh, I could never do that.

ARLES. Why not?

BERTHA. Well, I'd get the giggles, for one thing.

ARLES. Read at the top of the next page.

BERTHA. *(She reads.)* Well I don't...That's just...Have you ever done that?

ARLES. Well...

BERTHA. Arles!

ARLES. Read on.

BERTHA. *(She reads.)* And you got this from a preacher?

ARLES. There's nothing in there that's not part of a healthy sexual relationship between a husband and wife.

BERTHA. I don't know.

ARLES. Turn the page.

BERTHA. *(turns the page and is totally shocked)* Oh Lord, how did they manage that? *(She hands the book to **ARLES**.)* I've seen enough. I had no idea folks did that sort of thing.

ARLES. All the time.

BERTHA. And to think all these years I was married to a man whose bedroom manner was roll over and play dead. Why that sorry son-of...

ARLES. *(cutting **BERTHA** off)* Baby, Hank and Trudy are part of the past, and every time we bring them up, we go back there. We don't need to do that. We've got everything ahead of us. I promise you, this marriage is going to be different.

BERTHA. Well, all right. But if I'm going to do that...*(indicates a place in the book)*...then you need to get things rolling like it shows on page seventeen.

(He finds page seventeen.)

ARLES. I think I can oblige you.

BERTHA. My pleasures are important, too.

ARLES. I hear you, Baby.

BERTHA. I want to feel desired.

ARLES. Don't hold back.

BERTHA. And never taken for granted.

ARLES. Baby, Baby, Baby.

BERTHA. I want to be pursued.

ARLES. You want to be pursued?

BERTHA. I want to be pursued by you, and only you.

ARLES. You want to be pursued?

BERTHA. I want to be pursued.

(There is a short pause.)

ARLES. *(ARLES gets out of bed.)* Well, take off.

(ARLES tickles BERTHA and she gets out of bed. She runs a few steps. He follows. She runs a few more. He follows. She giggles and runs down the hall. He disappears after her. Pause. They appear again, ARLES chasing BERTHA.)

BERTHA. Arles, stop it. You are so silly. Arles, you're going to make me pee in my pants.

(He continues chasing her.)

ARLES. Don't fight it, Baby. It's bigger than the both of us.

(They disappear. We see parts of Bertha's clothing thrown onto the stage. BERTHA enters and ARLES chases her again, this time with his pants down around his ankles. They disappear again. ARLES runs into the room as if being chased, looks back. BERTHA follows a few steps behind scantily clad, showing a lot of leg. BERTHA giggles and chases him off. They exit. Lights fade to black as we hear music.)

The End

COSTUME PLOT

When all characters are played by two actors, one actor plays:

STAR BIRDFEATHER: In Act I and II, she wears a body length, loose-weaved vestment over a tie-dyed moomoo, half-size rose-colored lens sun glasses, flesh hose, sandals, and a blond wig of straight hair that reaches almost to her waist.

THURSTON WHEELIS: In Act I, Sc. 2, he wears round tortoise shell glasses, red and black plaid flannel shirt, faded denim bib overalls, flesh hose, black shoes.

ELMER WATKINS: In Act I, Sc.2, he wears a black "gimme" hat with "NRA" patch, dark blue windbreaker, rigged with quilted dark blue vest, all worn over THURSTON's plaid shirt, overalls, flesh hose and black shoes.

BERTHA BUMILLER: In Act I, Scene iii, she wears a dark brown bouffant-styled wig, patriotic earrings, large glasses with neck chain, patriotic print long-sleeve blouse, Kelly green polyester pants with matching vest, green and brown flats, and flesh hose. At the end of the scene she takes a large brown purse from an on-stage hat rack before exiting. In Act I, Scene iv, she enters with the purse. In Act II, Scene v, she wears white pants with matching vest, a pale print blouse, white flats, a wedding corsage, white earrings and the same wig and glasses with neck chain and flesh hose. Her wig, glasses, and shoes are preset at the top of Act II on one of two on-stage hat racks.

JOE BOB LIPSEY: In Act I, he wears magenta sun glasses, gold neck chain, much stomach padding, beige safari suit (jacket and pants), bright tropical print shirt rigged into jacket, white short socks and brown open-backed clogs. In Act II, he adds a queen's crown, cape and baldric sash.

PEARL BURRAS: In Act I, she wears a long blue flower print belted dress (old-lady type) with low-slung breast padding and butt padding, pearls, rigged to dress, black orthopedic shoes (old-lady shoes), flesh hose, hat with red, white and blue decoration, pearl cluster earrings, white gloves, cane, and black purse with a white lace handkerchief inside. In Act II, Scene iv, she wears a full-length chenille robe with dickey, plaid booties, mesh night cap and cane. Her robe is worn over Bertha's Act II, Scene v wedding outfit, and her booties over Bertha's Act II, v shoes.

R. R. SNAVELY: In both Acts, he wears full coveralls, madras plaid sports jacket, plaid bow tie, small straw hat with madras plaid band, and slip-on mesh shoes.

INITA GOODWIN: In Act II, Sc. 2, for her first entrance, she wears a red wig styled up, patriotic earrings, a square dancing outfit (separate top and skirt with petticoats), a purple and green letter jacket (letter 'T') that fits too snuggly, short white socks, and white athletic shoes. She carries on a pair of cowboy boots. For her second entrance, only her top half is costumed. For her third entrance she is wearing the cowboy boots but not the leather jacket.

LEONARD CHILDERS: In Act II, Sc. 2, he wears a grey wig, light blue western yolk suit (pants and jacket), white shirt and bolo tie rigged into the jacket, brown loafers, and flesh hose.

REVEREND STURGIS SPIKES: In Act II, Sc. 2, he wears a white three-piece suit, white shirt, black ribbon tie, white straw panama hat, glasses, American flag lapel pin, small grey mustache, white loafers, flesh hose.

When all characters are played by two actors, the other actor plays:

AMBER WINDCHIME: In Act I and II, she wears a large tie-dyed, peace-symbol T-shirt over psychedelic-patterned tights, large earrings, and moccasins. Her hair is brunette, long and straight with bangs.

ARLES STRUVIE: In Act I, he wears a Western yolk shirt (no fringe), black pants, black belt with small gold buckle, black cowboy boots, white socks, and a straw cowboy hat ("Fort Worth pinch"). He has a mustache. (In Act I, Scene ii, Arles may wear black slip-ons and no sox to accommodate the quick changes.) In Act II, he exchanges his Western yolk shirt to one with fringe. This "dressy" shirt, his hat and his mustache are preset at the top of Act II on one of two on-stage hat racks. (In Act II, Scene v, Arles may wear Stanley's Boots and Pants, but with the pants legs pulled over the boots

DIDI SNAVELY: In both Act I and II, she wears a clear plastic raincoat with red raindrop print, lined with camouflage print, patched with multi-colored gaff and electrical tape, clear plastic head bonnet lined with camouflage print, with frizzy dark hair at front and back, white ankle socks, slip-on "wedgie" sandals. (In Act I, Scene ii, Didi may go without her white socks to accommodate the quick change.)

PETEY FISK: In both Acts, he wears black pants (same as ARLES), waist-long blue denim coat, rigged to close askew, dark gray cap with ear flaps, rigged with Velcro patch at front, 4X6 cards rigged with Velcro to attach to cap, crudely imprinted with slogans like Save the Whales, Save the Dolphins, Save the Fire Ants, Save the Deer Ticks, Save the Scorpions, Save the Lemmings, brown loafers and white socks.

CHARLENE BUMILLER: In Act I, Sc. 3, she wears a page-boy dark blond wig, pink hair clips, pink-framed large-lens glasses, a pink patterned maternity top over pink pants with hip and butt padding, pink and white athletic shoes, and white socks. She is at least 8 months pregnant.

STANLEY BUMILLER: In Act I and Act II, Sc. 2, he wears a black T-shirt and black jeans with a silver-and-turquoise belt buckle, black "biker" boots with pants tucked into boots, a black bandanna tied around one boot, a black bandanna tied around his head, and white socks. (In Act II, Scene iv, the belt buckle is worn over Arles' belt and is removable.

VERA CARP: In Act I, she wears a peach-colored satin slip with bra, peach-colored satin house coat, open at front with peach marabou feather trim, blond wig, white "cat eye" glasses, earrings, knee-high hose (no white socks), peach sandals with marabou feather accent. In Act II, she wears a stylish peach-colored summer suit, with white purse and heels, a white pill box hat and knee-high hose.

HELEN BEDD: In Act II, Sc. 2, for her first entrance, she wears a black wig, styled up, earrings, short skirt, elastic girdle with hip padding, short-sleeve, collared blouse with breast padding, panty hose, and clear acrylic high-heel sandals (Frederick's of Hollywood). She carries on a pair of cowboy boots. For her second entrance, she is wearing a square dancing outfit with petticoats and the cowboy boots.

GARLAND POTEET: In Act II, Sc. 2, only his upper half is costumed in a khaki uniform shirt, embroidered with name and "soda" logo, and a cloth wide-brim hat with band of bottle caps.

PROPERTY PLOT

SET PROPS & FURNITURE:
Two Tables and **Four Chairs** and **Two Hat Racks** and an old fashioned cabinet floor model **Console Radio**, gutted and fitted with a speaker and interior light, and a Food Booth **Window Unit** fit into the center wall just behind the radio console that opens and closes from off-stage. The window's cover is made of two horizontal panels that are hinged with a piano hinge to collapse out and rest on top of the radio console forming a shelf in front of the window that is supported solely by the radio. The window cover is rigged to travel on tracks on the window sides and is raised and lowered by pulleys from off-stage.

SET DRESSING:
Various pieces of clothing on the hat racks, including Bertha's purse, which is preset at the top of the show and Arles' and Bertha's costume pieces (see costume plot), which are preset at the top of Act II.

In Act II, Sc. 2, there is a men's and a women's restroom sign that are spring loaded and pop out from the walls stage right and left and can be retracted from off-stage at the end of the scene and a sign that flies in over the food booth window and out at the top and bottom of the scene that reads "Hot to Trot Catering."

HAND PROPS:
All props are mimed except for costume props like purses, a cane for Pearl, and a practical bull horn that Vera wears on a strap around her neck in Act II, Sc 2.

GROUNDPLAN

(Act II, Sc. 2 signs) ⇒ Men   Act II, Sc. 2   Women

Window opens for Food Booth

Hat rack

RADIO

Hat rack

Table & Chairs

Table and Chairs

Note: The chairs are rearranged to form car seats and the head and foot of a bed.

Hat rack

RADIO

Hat rack

Lupe's Car (II, 1)

Bed (II, 4 & 5)

Star and Amber's
Car (I, 1)

Pearl's
Car (II, 1)

MORE TUNA AVAILABLE FROM SAMUEL FRENCH

A TUNA CHRISTMAS
Jaston Williams, Joe Sears and Ed Howard

Holiday Comedy / 2m, or Flexible Casting / Simple Set

In this hilarious sequel to *Greater Tuna*, it's Christmas in the third smallest town in Texas. Radio station OKKK news personalities Thurston Wheelis and Arles Struvie report on various Yuletide activities, including hot competition in the annual lawn display contest. In other news, voracious Joe Bob Lipsey's production of *A Christmas Carol* is jeopardized by unpaid electric bills. Many colorful Tuna denizens, some you will recognize from *Greater Tuna* and some appearing here for the first time, join in the holiday fun. *A Tuna Christmas* is a total delight for all seasons, whether performed by two quick changing comedians as on Broadway or by twenty or more. Production requirements are minimal, making the play suitable for school and community producers as well as large venues. Audiences who have and who have not seen *Greater Tuna* will enjoy this laugh filled evening.

SAMUELFRENCH.COM

MORE TUNA AVAILABLE FROM SAMUEL FRENCH

TUNA DOES VEGAS
Jaston Williams, Joe Sears and Ed Howard

Comedy / 2m / Ints, Exts

In the hilarious new installment from the legendary *Greater Tuna* creative team, *Tuna Does Vegas* re-unites the lovable and eccentric characters from the 'third smallest town in Texas' as they take a rambling romp in Sin City. The hilarity begins when oddball-conservative radio host Arles Struvie announces on air that he and his wife Bertha Bumiller are heading to Vegas to renew their wedding vows...but everyone in Tuna, Texas goes along for the ride! Written by Jaston Williams, Joe Sears and Ed Howard, *Tuna Does Vegas* will feature the favorite characters from the award-winning "*Greater Tuna*" productions with some new characters too! —all staged under the directorial hand of Mr. Howard.

Tuna Does Vegas balances as both an affectionate comment on small-town life and attitudes as well a hilarious satire of the same. The eclectic band of citizens that make up this town are portrayed by only Mr. Sears and Mr. Williams, making this send-up on life in rural America even more delightful as they depict all of the inhabitants of Tuna - men, women, as well as Vegas showgirls, Elvis impersonators and more!